EVERYBODY LOBBIES

The Art of
Ethical and Effective Lobbying

By Stan and Gail Long

ISBN 1-932203-34-6

Published by:
Express Media
1419 Donelson Pike
Nashville, TN 37217

Table of Contents

A DEDICATION AND A THANK YOU

There are many ways an author can dedicate a book. There are usually many people in a profession or a trade that share experiences and knowledge, thus deserving well-earned recognition. We are grateful for the help of those holding public office, heading governmental departments, and particularly, practicing lobbyists who have already earned distinguished records in lobbying. Their interest and advice contributed greatly to our book on lobbying.

One, deserving special mention is the Pennsylvania Association For Government Relations. We asked for and received permission to quote their Guidelines to Lobbyists, one of the finest yet published. It appears on the following pages.

Guidelines to Lobbyists

The Pennsylvania Association for Government Relations believes that effective government depends on the greatest possible participation of those being governed. At the state level, such participation focuses on the legislative and executive branches where professional and citizen lobbyists drawn from every major discipline represent literally every segment of society and every sector of the economy.

The Association further believes that the heavy responsibility of the professional lobbyist, functioning in the eye of public opinion, requires standards of ethical behavior beyond those generally accepted by a free and moral society.

The Association therefore, offers the following guidelines which it urges be observed by its members and all those whose professional objectives are to influence state public policy decisions.

- It is the system of representative government we enjoy that makes possible the practice of lobbying. The professional lobbyist, while keeping the interest of employer or client in a position of primacy, will temper the advocacy role with proper consideration for the general public interest.

- The professional lobbyist will protect confidences not only those of the employer or client, and also those of elected and appointed officials of government and professional colleagues.

- The professional lobbyist will always deal in accurate, current and factual information, whether it is being reported to the employer or client, government officials, the media or professional colleagues, and will not engage in misrepresentation of any nature.

- The professional lobbyist will acquire enough knowledge of public issues to be able to fairly present all points of view.

- The professional lobbyist will avoid conflicts of interest, not only with the interests of the employer or client, but also those of colleagues pursuing the same or similar objectives, and where conflict is unavoidable, will communicate the facts fully and freely to those affected.

- The professional lobbyist will comply with the laws and regulations governing lobbying, as well as the standards of conduct applying to officials and staff of the General Assembly and the Executive Branch, and will strive to go one step further and function in a manner that goes beyond these official enactments and promulgations.

- The personal conduct of the professional lobbyist should not bring discredit to the profession, government, or individual colleagues.

- The professional lobbyist will refrain from any form of discrimination which is legally proscribed or simply generally recognized as such.

- The priority goal of the professional lobbyist should be to increase public understanding of the process. This objective should be pursued in every possible way - public appearances, media contracts, articles in company and other publications, and contacts in the normal course of everyday life.

- The professional lobbyist should constantly strive to upgrade the necessary skills by every means available, continuing formal education, attendance at meetings and seminars, and participation in ad hoc groups with like-minded colleagues.

SECTION 1

The Art of Lobbying. Seven Good Reasons Explored

An introduction to the ancestry of lobbying, the practices of lobbying in the past, and providing a foundation throughout the following related subjects:

1. Why are lobbyists needed, **now** as history proves they have always been.

2. The reasons for choosing lobbying as a profession.

3. A successful lobbyists' basic characteristics.

4. Important governmental procedures outlined.

5. The various interest groups competing for attention.

6. Implementing public relations with lobbying activity.

7. Association lobbying

Chapter I – WHAT THIS BOOK IS ALL ABOUT

Then the serpent said to Eve "..., and you will be like God, knowing good and evil". (Gen. 3:5).

And so, according to some, was the art of lobbying born. Interestingly, it has never lost this evil connotation. It is still maligned by many private individuals, members of the media and elected officials. Individuals decry what they feel to be the unfair advantage of special interest groups. Reporters delight in writing stories recounting the "dirty tricks" of lobbyists who are suspected of financial wrong doing, and legislators pass laws to limit the powers of lobbyists. However, few, if any, of these people fully understand either the basic function or the techniques of lobbying. Nor do they seem to grasp the fact that lobbying as an art is practiced by people in all walks of life.

Without knowing it, children are excellent lobbyists. "But Mother, everyone is going. I'll be ruined if I have to stay home". More to the point, members of the clergy, doctors, those who write and answer editorials, and even elected officials themselves practice the art of lobbying. That is, they practice their constitutionally guaranteed rights of freedom of speech and to petition the government. For that is what lobbying is basically all about; the attempt, through reasoned argument, to persuade another that your stand is the best, or the correct one.

Granted, there are techniques and rules of the game that need to be learned. Yet, they are not hidden in some mysterious cave, or available only to those who go through ritual initiation into the secret order of lobbyists. These techniques are available to any one who is willing to spend the time and energy necessary to master them. Once learned, they can be used to help persuade neighbors, committees, local city councils, church boards, and even children.

It is the purpose of this book to help the interested person become conversant with, and adept at, those basic lobbying techniques. Not that everyone who reads this book will become a professional lobbyist (or even want to), but most individuals face situations where knowing how to make a clear and forceful presentation is essential. On the other hand, this book presents useful tools for those people who find themselves in the position of carrying out the duties of a professional lobbyist, such as directors of associations, members of the government affairs department of a large corporation, or a concerned citizen.

As was stated earlier, the techniques of lobbying are useful in a wide variety of situations. However, the terms lobbyist and lobbying have historically been limited to the government decision making process. For purposes of clarity and simplicity, the illustrations used in this book are in that context.

The term lobbying became part of our political vocabulary around 1830. At that time, manufacturers and other large industries began to send representatives to Washington, D.C., as well as various state capitols. It was the function of these representatives to try to influence lawmakers to pass legislation favorable to their employers. In order to get the legislators attention, these representatives would gather (loiter) in the lobbies that adjoined the legislative meeting halls, waiting to speak to a law maker before or after a session. The popular press began referring to these people as lobby waiters, or lobbyists. As the role of the government grew, so did the number of lobbyists waiting in those lobbies.

Consequently, the lobbies became so congested they were placed off limits to all but members of the legislative body. At that point, lobbyists began to develop and refine the techniques that are the integral components of lobbying today. Therefore, while the original practice no longer exists, the term has remained.

In the same way, as the role of government has increased, and as it has expanded its power over the lives of individuals, interest groups, and businesses, the need for lobbyists has also increased. Concurrently, the art of lobbying has become more clearly defined. Even though public relations, the law, teaching, and lobbying are all involved with communication, each exists within its own milieu. Public relations, as the name suggests, involves creating a favorable public image for a product, candidate or issue. The law is concerned with adjudicating and interpreting the existing rules of society. It views compromise as a last resort. Education involves the absorption of knowledge for later use. Lobbying, on the other hand, revolves around the creation of the law, and often equates success with compromise. Additionally, it is aimed at the immediate use of the facts presented. This clarification of the definition of lobbying has been coupled with a greater sophistication of techniques.

Lobbyists have become more adept at research, oral and written communication. Those who use these techniques well, and who have earned the respect of officials and their colleagues, often times find themselves being sought out as expert witnesses. It is not unusual for a committee or agency actively to seek the opinion of such a lobbyist on pending legislation or a proposed policy. Obviously, a lobbyist who garners this type of respect is more effective for his client. And that is the bottom line; pragmatically to represent the ideas, wishes, and needs of others in the exercise of their rights to speak and to petition the government.

In essence the lobbyist becomes a "bridge" between the individual and those who are political decision-makers. Within this context, the best interest of the client must always be the lobbyist's primary concern. In other words, a lobbyist must use all of his or her research and communication skills to present the client's point of view on the impending legislation or policy. It is the lobbyist's responsibility to make sure that the political decision makers have all the pertinent data as to the ramifications of possible actions; that any necessary compromises do not work against the best interest of the client; and that the client fully understands the process and the reasons for its outcome.

> However, as to the matter of lobbying, some believe that term implies something rather ominous and maybe devious and harmful to society. Others will use the word, "Legislative Advocate" or "Information Provider", or you name it. The fact of the matter is, all of us, in some form or another, do some lobbying during different stages of our lives or professional careers. And we don't necessarily call ourselves lobbyists.
> We just call it "Community Involvement."
> A democracy, as you know, requires that involvement of its citizens and if you don't participate and provide information and speak to the issues that affect you, your values, or the things that you feel are important, you are not a responsible, participating citizen.
>
> Frank Mesple: practicing lobbyist

Not only must a client understand the reasons for the results of a particular lobbying effort; he must also understand the reasons for deciding whether to undertake such a project in the first place. There are four basic considerations that determine the feasibility of any lobbying project. At the outset, a lobbyist should never accept a project that is in direct conflict with the interests of an existing client or the lobbyist's personal principles. To do so would diminish the lobbyist's effectiveness for both clients. In addition, such a conflict of interest could generate lasting negative impressions on the political decision-makers that would be involved. Consequently, the next time this lobbyist had to come before this same group, his effectiveness would be greatly diminished. No lobbyist can afford that type of reception.

Along with the question of possible conflicts of interest, a lobbyist considers the likelihood of success before deciding whether to undertake a particular project. It is not so much a question of guaranteed success, but rather the question of guaranteed failure that a lobbyist must address. There must be some hope that at least part of the client's position can be incorporated into the final law or policy. For example, even though the lobbyist might agree with a potential client's desire to see a law enacted that would ban sex on TV, such a law would have practically no chance of passing - in any form. While the attempt to pass such legislation would afford the client a platform for this particular idea, its primary result would be a waste of time and money. Obviously, a lobbyist who accepted mainly "lost causes" would soon lose his effectiveness.

Once it has been decided that no conflict of interest exists, and that there is some hope for the client's stand, the third question to be addressed is that of money. Does the client have sufficient resources for the lobbyist's fee and the other expenditures that are part of such an effort? It might be decided, for instance, that it would be essential for the client, through the lobbyist, to contribute to the reelection campaign of one or more office holders. This could mean the purchasing of a number of tickets for campaign dinners. These dinners usually cost between $200 to $1000 per person. Does the client have the necessary funds? Also, does he have the time and energy necessary to attend these dinners with the lobbyist, if that strategy is deemed important? Are there funds available for the lobbyist to travel to the seat of government? What about publicity? All of these expenditures can be incurred during a successful lobbying project. Therefore, the lobbyist and the client must be absolutely certain about the size of the budget and the availability of funds to meet that budget.

If it is decided that there are sufficient funds for the type of lobbying effort that will be required, one more issue needs to be addressed. Are the results of this lobbying effort going to work for or against the client's best interest? If the client is an individual or industry who must depend upon the good will of the public, might this project have a negative effect on the public's perception of the client? Is it possible the client's stand on this issue could put him permanently at odds with other political decision-makers; decision-makers he may have to come before at some future time. If either of these two results seem to be possible, it is the lobbyist's duty to apprise the client of this. However, only the client can make the final determination as to whether the risk is worth taking.

Once the decision has been made to undertake a particular project, it becomes the task of the lobbyist to utilize all of his skills and talents on behalf of the client. The rest of this book covers in detail those talents and skills.

Chapter II -   WHY THERE IS A NEED FOR LOBBYISTS

"So your mind gets changed. A good lobbyist will help you to change it. That's his business"

Having introduced the concept of lobbying; what it is and what it is not, it is time to take a look at the question of "Why is there a need for lobbyists?" The simplest and most direct answer is that every piece of legislation, and every administrative policy, is going to affect someone. In some cases positive effects result, and in others negative outcomes occur. However, those who are impacted by such a law or policy are faced with one of two realities.

In most cases those who are the targets of the proposal do not even know it exists. Most individuals who work in occupations that can be impacted by government rarely have the time, or in some cases, the ability to keep informed of such actions. The same is true of those whose civil rights might be denied them, or whose recreational pursuits could put them in contact with the government Most interest groups are developed because of the needs of these people. Lobbyists, therefore, are needed to encourage the positive and discourage the negative.

> **Let me begin** by saying to you, very sincerely, that I think it is extremely important that we all understand that lobbying and moving forward with your point of view is an extremely important activity, because we, as members of legislative bodies, and others who have responsibility for making public policy, and making decisions regarding public policies, often do not have the time to deal with the countless issues in depth. We are forced to make decisions so there must be a great deal of reliance on those who are experts, those who have the expertise in more intricate and detailed fashion, regarding either a piece of legislation or some issue requiring a public decision. We have to rely on the kind of information that is brought to us by those who are experts.
>
> **Councilman David Cunningham, Los Angeles**

What are some of the negatives that can result from a law or a policy? Assume that a lobbyist's major concern is that a proposed law would mean the financial ruin of his client. Unless the client is a major employer or contributor to election campaigns, using that fact as an argument against the bill would probably not be particularly effective. There is a need to show the legislators that the law would have widespread negative effects.

Since the lobbyist cannot fabricate a problem that could not possibly exist, he finds other legitimate reasons for opposing it. In all probability any law that could cause the financial ruin of a client could have other far-reaching effects. It becomes the job of the lobbyist to decide which of these negative scenarios would most likely generate the desired result - i.e. the death or amendment of the bill. Once that decision is made, he works his presentation around these assumptions.

Although the legislators may be familiar with the general areas involved in the bill, there is still a need to rely on lobbyists for the specific data they can provide. Legislators and their staff do not have time to research each bill in detail. Therefore, those lobbyists whose clients will be effected by the proposal strives to give office holders an in depth view of some of the consequences of a bill, as it relates to these clients.

This need for specific data becomes quite important when one realizes that those who make public policy strive to balance the needs of the individuals or groups being represented by a lobbyist with the needs of the public. Therefore, one of the most effective arguments that can be made by a lobbyist - if it can be done legitimately- is that the proposal would create an economic hardship on the public.

Elected officials are wary of making the electorate unhappy, especially by costing them money.
For instance, the auto industry was able to delay for years the required installation of air bags, by pointing out that they would increase the price of a car.

An even better example involves a 1973 proposal by the Environmental Protection Agency. The EPA decided that the best way to reduce pollution in Los Angeles was to reduce the number of cars on the road. In order to accomplish this, it was decided to place an annual tax of $430 on every parking space, both on and off the street. The only exceptions allowed would be for churches and residences. This meant that local governments and businesses would have been required to pay $430 for every space they provided, as would have hospitals, shopping malls, schools, amusement parks, etc. Obviously, this tax would have been passed on to the consumer in the form of higher prices in the private sector and higher property taxes in the public sector.

Even though at its own public hearings, held in Los Angeles, every speaker was against the proposal, the agency decided that its plan was the best course of action. In addition, a joint lobbying effort by the parking industry and the city of Los Angeles was unsuccessful in getting the EPA to change its mind. However, when these two entities turned their efforts toward Congress; the outcome was far different.

Every parking lot and garage in the greater Los Angeles area was provided with thousands of fact sheets and preaddressed post cards. These were distributed to patrons as they drove into the location. Once individuals became familiar with the EPA proposal, the post cards and phone calls began to reach members of the California delegation in the House and the Senate, as well as the national director of the EPA. Literally hundreds of thousands of such cards and calls reached these people. Not one constituent response favored the plan. Members of Congress, realizing that the public knew Congress had the power to stop the plan, went with the desires of the people.

During this lobbying effort, there was never any mention of the probable economic hardships the plan would have caused the parking industry. There didn't have to be. Through the use of constituent mail and phone calls, elected politicians were persuaded to pass a law prohibiting the EPA from putting its plan into effect, and requiring Congressional approval for any such future plans. While this example involves a major industry dealing with the federal level of the government, the same strategy can be just as effective at the state or local level.

Assume that the only client a particular lobbyist has is a small local association of people who own bed and breakfast inns. There is an attempt by the city council to impose a stiff bed tax on these establishments. An effective lobbyist is able to get the measure defeated by pointing out the long range financial consequences of such a law, by showing the council members that the tax would mean fewer visitors to the city, because not as many people would be able to afford the room rates. This would mean fewer people eating in the city's restaurants, using its taxis, buying souvenirs, all of which would mean a loss in tax revenue.

At the same time, the lobbyist realizes that any issue can be politically damaging to members of the legislature. So, while these decision-makers rely heavily on the material presented by lobbyists, the one who is representing the inn owners is very careful to use good, analytical objective research. As a result of the lobbyist's efforts, the council rejects the tax. Not only is the client pleased, but also others, who might be facing a similar battle, are now aware of his lobbying expertise. He may be confronted with the happy prospect of turning clients away. However, not all proposals have such an obvious economic consequence.

Could there still be a need to lobby? Most assuredly. In some instances it is quite legitimate to point out that the bill in question flies in the face of traditional American values. It could be something as fundamental as the conflict between those who favor abortion and those who do not. It might be as heated as were the arguments between the supporters of the war against Iraq and those who feared the consequences of such an engagement. Even though both sides based their arguments on the same value, their love for their country, they struggled to enact differing methods to put that value into practice. This points up a very frustrating problem in our society.

Often times two diametrically opposed groups use the same values to support their point of view. For instance, both sides in the school prayer proposals base their arguments on the values of tradition and freedom of religion. Those who favor prayer in public schools point out that when public education began in this country, the Bible was the basic textbook. Parents were concerned that their children learn to read the scriptures as well as be able to do basic arithmetic. On the other hand, those who oppose the plan, point to the traditional separation of church and state as called for in the First Amendment.

The appeal to values can also be used against a bill that is financially injurious to a client. A lobbyist might generate a strategy based on stressing the negative social consequences of any such proposals, especially consequences to the specific constituents of the legislators involved. This tactic is particularly effective in dealing with members of the committee to which the bill has been assigned. However, the lobbyist must be able to show clearly how the voters will be hurt by the passage of the bill. For example, those who favor abortion on demand, and are lobbying against an anti-abortion statute are much more likely to discuss the concept of freedom of choice for pregnant women, rather than the economic advantage of such a policy to those who run facilities where abortions are performed. In like manner, those who favor prayer in schools, present arguments that involve questions of religious freedom, and freedom of speech rather than attempting to show that those individuals who have had some personal exposure to religious values tend to be more conscientious and honest employees, especially if the client is a major employer.

Values issues can be frustrating, but they can also be immensely challenging and rewarding. Additionally, not all value issues involve obvious economic consequences. There are times when extremely dedicated people clash over a values question purely on the basis of what is good for the environment, such as off-road vehicles being allowed in the deserts of the Southwest. Similar clashes over values were involved in the fight over the Equal Rights Amendment. Although other types of arguments may arise with specific bills or policies; most lobbying efforts revolve around the question of economic hardship, to others, as well as the client, or a conflict of values. The successful lobbyist is sufficiently prepared to know which argument would be the most effective in diminishing any negative consequences to his client.

The other side of a lobbyist's job is to encourage passage of legislation or policies that would have positive results for a client. Generally any bill or policy that is important enough to lobby, is viewed differently by those who might be impacted by it. If there are those who are opposed to the measure, it is fairly certain that there are those who favor it. The passage of this type of law is personally very important to any lobbyist. The more positive results a client can see, the more secure his position becomes. As a lobbyist is able to achieve more and more favorable legislation, his clients take on more stature within the entire public sector, not just the legislative branch.

As their stature and clout increase, so does the lobbyist's. Others who need lobbying help hear of him, and hopefully, begin to seek him out. This expands the reputation of the lobbyist and the client, giving both a stronger standing when dealing with governmental decision-makers.

Chapter III - WHY BECOME A LOBBYIST

Imagine being paid to do all the things you love to do. If you enjoy the demands and the fun, then lobbying is for you.

For many Americans, the word lobbyist conjures up images of bribery, conspiracy, or other kinds of underhanded activities. At the very least, lobbyist and lobbying fit into the category of what semanticist S. I. Hayakawa termed Snarl Words. These are words that stir up resentments and bring snarls to ones lips. In contrast to these terms are what he called Purr Words, those that soothe and make one feel good, such as Mom and apple pie. If these negative perceptions of lobbying exist, and judging by the popular press they certainly seem to, then why should an individual want to become a lobbyist?

I think that young people might very well consider a career as a lobbyist. Particularly, if they can do it in connection with something in which they deeply believe. But their services shouldn't just be for sale. The good and the effective lobbyist, as I said, operates in a goldfish bowl and uses persuasion. He gets to know the legislator and the executives and he gains their confidence by providing solid fact and evidence for his cause. He also tells frankly, the other side of the picture.

Congressman Jerry Voorhis California

This is an interesting question, which is best answered by fully understanding the types of activities that are part of the art of lobbying: research, analysis, and communication being the most fundamental. Many individuals exercise one or more of these activities on a regular basis. It might be at a city council meeting, where parents are trying to persuade the council to put a stop light in front of a school. It might be negotiating with one's boss for a pay raise, or a promotion. It might be at homeowners' association meeting, where members are trying to decide on their annual budget. In these three cases, and countless others of a similar nature, those who actively seek a specific goal first research the necessary data, analyze it, and then communicate their conclusions. In other words most individuals are lobbyists to one degree or another.

However, it is those few who truly enjoy these types of activities who find lobbying to be a rewarding experience. And that is the primary reason to become an amateur or professional lobbyist, because an individual enjoys the challenges that are presented, and the methods used to meet those challenges.

The practice of law is a good example of a profession that meets the above criteria. Even though lobbying is basically a counterpoint of the legal profession, in that lawyers work with established laws, while lobbyists are a part of the law-making process, a working knowledge of the law is also a major asset. A lawyer who becomes a lobbyist, or who even has an occasion to lobby a particular piece of legislation, holds an advantage over less knowledgeable opponents. He has a clearer understanding of the language used by lawmakers, and is more conversant with possible legal loopholes. Lastly, lawyers are trained in the arts of research, analysis and the ability to communicate information from a specific point of view.

On the other hand, those lawyers who choose to enter the field of lobbying, rather than practice law, are not guaranteed success. A lawyer who infrequently takes on a case involving a direct matter of legislative advocacy may find himself confused and frustrated. This is usually because there has not been time or opportunity to do the type of preparation that is described in this book. Nor does legal training automatically qualify one for the practice of legislative advocacy.

Whereas lawyers are generally taught that winning an outright victory is their paramount duty to the client, lobbyists learn that compromise is often more of a victory than is getting everything a client wants on a particular bill. Lobbyists realize the need to develop on going relationships with public officials, since in the long run, a compromise may save the client a defeat on a later matter. As such, those lawyers who can alter their thinking processes stand an excellent chance of becoming effective lobbyists.

Another logical argument for entering this field is that there are so many opportunities that can relate to previous experience. While legislative houses are usually organized on a geographical basis, lobbyists represent people directly in terms of their economic or other interests. The lobbyist speaks for people such as manufacturers, steelworkers, veterans, or teachers. As long as this type of functional representation is not abused, it is a highly necessary supplement to geographical representation. Let us say, for example, that an individual grew up on a family farm. She has some experience in, considerable empathy for and understanding of farming and other types of agricultural pursuits. One of the most important lobbies in Washington is the agricultural lobby. It makes more sense for someone with such a background to represent growers, or farmers, or co-ops, than for someone whose background is devoid of any type of agricultural experience. By the same token, a person who has an industrial background, working in a factory or in an electronics laboratory brings to the lobbying arena a valuable experience, which can be used most properly in those areas of endeavor. As can be seen from the above examples, different types of experiences whether based on one's occupation or life style; furnish an individual with a sound introduction into the art

However, experience in a field is not a sufficient reason for representing a particular client. No one should undertake to represent a group or a cause in which he has little or no interest or belief. It is almost a truism that a successful lobbyist must believe in what and who he endeavors to represent. Those who become professional lobbyists tend to adhere to the idea that within a democratic system, the individual can make a difference. Opportunities to represent the interests of those whose cause one believes in exist at all levels of government. It may take diligence to locate those with similar interests and/or philosophy, but an individual who truly wants to make a difference through lobbying finds the search highly rewarding.

In addition to the opportunity to represent a particular interest, an individual may consider entering the field of lobbying because of its possible financial benefits. A good lobbyist can command attractive fees for his efforts because he earns them. This is a strong incentive, whether the lobbying account is based upon a monthly retainer; a straight assignment basis, an agreed upon figure, with payments being made periodically, or on a per diem basis. Any one of these arrangements can be financially rewarding. Lobbyists who seek more job security may join a particular corporation as an in-house advocate. On the other hand, those who enjoy risk taking may wish to start their own practice. It is always best however, for an independent lobbyist to develop more than one account, so that if something turns sour, he has another source of income.

While having multiple accounts is desirable, they must be carefully chosen. They must not conflict with each other nor cast an unfavorable light upon the other by reason of common representation. A lobbyist who is well prepared, and who communicates effectively can be as busy as he wants to be. As government becomes more involved in our daily lives, the need for having one's voice heard also grows. This growing involvement of the government points to another reason for selecting lobbying as one's life work.

The field is not as crowded as are so many others. When one considers the fact that the Congress, fifty state legislatures, and thousands of local councils and boards are generating tens of thousands of laws a year, the opportunities in lobbying are staggering. There are over 15,000 individuals in Washington D.C. who function as lobbyists. They address the needs of clients who may be impacted by one or more of the over 22,000 bills that are introduced into the U.S. Congress each year. Those who love the type of activities that are common to lobbying have an open market for their skills.

A good lobbyist who has already " earned his stripes" or who is making a valiant first effort finds himself sought out by prospective clients. But, to be successful as a lobbyist, the individual must prove himself, by his demeanor and ability to organize and present his client's case. Additionally, he gradually needs to develop a portfolio of successful case histories. This takes time, as does anything of real value. It doesn't happen overnight, but one answer that can be given on the "why" question is the fact that it is do-able.

Notice the words "prove himself" in the previous paragraph. Many make the mistake of over-selling their ability to perform. They may do so without malice or intent to defraud but when it comes time to deliver - the delivery of results just does not occur. Let this happen often enough, and the lobbyist is out of the profession. Others who have given lobbying a bad name have been nothing more than fast talkers who claim all kind of connections and who lead a client to believe that all he needs to do is pay a healthy retainer and they can "fix it for you".

The "fixer" is not a true lobbyist. Basically all he does is give lobbying in general a bad name. We have all seen this character around. He brags about his friend who is on the City Council or in the legislature. He throws names around hoping the client is impressed not with what he knows, but rather whom he knows. He may even have a shirt tail relationship with someone, but if a "fix" rather than a sincere compelling presentation of a case is desired, then both the client and his so-called counsel risk losing their case, and all future credibility. There are few short cuts to success in the ethical act of lobbying.

One hears about the I.O.U.'S that lobbyists are supposed to collect as a result of favors or contributions that are made to office holders. Basically what they collect, and truthfully all they have any reason to expect to collect, is an open door to future discussions. More than that should not be expected. The idea that lobbyists should not expect more than an open door and an objective hearing on the part of the legislature leads to another reason why some people elect to the pursue the art of lobbying.

They find it is possible to have a challenging and rewarding career and still remain ethical. A large number of lobbyists were first attracted to the profession by the fact that they could have a genuine influence on our government and still maintain their own integrity. Obviously, there are public office holders who are corruptible. They make the news on a daily basis. However, what is encouraging is that the vast majority of those individuals who hold political office do not make the news because of their corruption.

Even though the possibility to damage the system is always present, most of those who are within it, elected and appointed alike, manage to remain ethical and honest. For those of a like mind who seek to have a say within that system, this is an encouraging reality. As legislators and members of the executive branch become more willing to address their own corruptibility by passing laws that limit campaign contributions and create codes of ethical behavior, the opportunities for those who truly love to lobby, to do the research, the analysis and the communicating will continue to increase.

Why be a lobbyist? Let's answer that question, by asking another one. What is one of the main reasons democracy continues to grow and function? One of the major factors is the fundamental right of free speech. Individuals in a democracy are free to praise, and free to criticize. They are free to argue and free to plead. For those who truly believe in the system, one of the most effective means of preserving it is to preserve free speech, and free access to those who govern us. Lobbyists are supremely important in this endeavor. It is vital that all that wish representation has the opportunity to be represented. The more lobbyists there are the more people and groups can be represented, and the more our governmental leaders are required to listen to the voices of the people.

In the long run, there is no one answer to the question of why become a lobbyist. But there are compelling reasons for those who like the type of work that is involved in being an effective lobbyist. It's a challenging career. It doesn't become a run of the mill job, and if a lobbyist is worth his fees, he is going to have plenty of exciting work to do on behalf of his clients. Remember, imagination, skill, honesty, and ethics can all work together.

` ` ` `

Chapter IV - CHARACTERISTICS OF A SUCCESSFUL LOBBYIST

> "In my senior year in high school, we had an aptitude test. I walked into the room; there were three things on a table, a bottle of scotch, a deck of cards, and a Bible. I was told to go about my business and select those things that interested me, they would let me know what I was good at after I did it. The first thing I did was grab the bottle of scotch, and look at it, tested the color, smelled the aroma and the person behind the magical desk said, 'He may be a drunk'. I put that down and went to the cards. I picked them up and shuffled them and knew right away that there were 52, and he said 'Oh my God, a card shark'. And last, I picked up the Bible and I opened it and began reading from the 23rd Psalm, and they said, 'You are a lobbyist'. And thus it was. And I am a lobbyist".
>
> **Scott Harvey**

Not everyone lobbies effectively. Knowing the techniques, having the contacts, even having clients does not guarantee success. As with any profession there are special attributes that predispose certain people to success and others to failure. A prospective neurosurgeon who was "all thumbs" would probably be well advised to try a field of medicine that demands less manual dexterity. In like manner, those who would lobby successfully must possess specific attributes and personality traits. Probably the most important of these is an even temperament.

It is essential that a lobbyist be patient. Time and time again situations arise that demand a calm and tolerant response. There is always the one member of the committee who never listens, and, therefore, asks the exact question that was just answered. There may be the client whose ignorance of government procedures makes him fearful and anxious, and, therefore, in need of constant reassurance. Some client's overblown self-image can threaten the lobbyist's relationship with the public official involved. Finding himself caught between the two sides the lobbyist must exercise great restraint in soothing both. Sometimes a staff member or a secretary feels that his/her position excuses, or even justifies, rude and brusque behavior. In dealing with people like this, patience is the best weapon, but it is not the only one.

A successful lobbyist must also be assertive, positive, and enthusiastic He must know what it is his client wants, and work toward those goals. He cannot be aggressive in manner, but he must be assertive. Aggression is used by those who do not have a solid grasp of their own facts or who see themselves as unable to compete intellectually with others. Those who are assertive have a firm case, which they know well. Their demeanor is positive but not overbearing. They are confident of their ability to compete with other lobbyists who are interested in the same policy. The following two illustrations help to clarify the difference.

Chairman Baumgarten has obviously not been listening. He suddenly asks a question. The same question that was just answered. How the lobbyist responds has a major impact on his chances for success.

(1) "Mr. Chairman, you obviously have not
listened to a word I said. Don't forget,
my client swings a lot of weight at election time. You'd
better pay closer attention to what's going on here."

(2) "Mr. Chairman, this part of the bill is the
main cause of our concern, so let me see
if I can clarify my answer to that question."

Obviously, the first illustration is somewhat overdrawn.
However, placing the two examples together does point up
the difference between these two approaches.

They also show the positive nature of a successful
lobbyist; those who are patient, tolerant, assertive and
positive tend to be the type of person others want to be
around. Approaching his client, the committee, or whoever is
involved in the project in a positive manner, tends to elicit a
like response. If, for instance, a staff member could give an
appointment to only one of two lobbyists, one of whom
exemplified the above traits, and the other who tended to be
negative and cynical, it seems obvious that the one chosen
would be the one who fits the profile of the successful
lobbyist.

However, temperament alone does not guarantee
success. Those lobbyists who are most often sought out are
those who also display integrity, truthfulness, and honesty.
On a very basic level, most people do not want to associate
with a person whose actions and motives are open to
suspicion. This is true of both clients and office holders. An
individual who suggests bribing an office holder may attract

a certain type of client, but his professional life will be quite short. As other politicians become aware of this attitude, access disappears. Without access to office holders and their staffs, lobbyists generally become ex lobbyists. With the press giving lobbyists and their activities so much coverage, it is vital to avoid even the appearance of wrongdoing.

Basically, a lobbyist's product is himself. As with any other product, consumers want to see it as unflawed. Products that do not perform as advertised or that are harmful to consumers are usually taken out of the market. Therefore, possessing integrity, honesty and truthfulness gives the lobbyist's efforts more validity and, consequently, more credibility. When an office holder knows that a lobbyist's word can be trusted, he is much more likely to accept what that lobbyist has to say. In the same vein, clients are more apt to hire him and to recommend him to others.

After an individual has been hired to lobby for a particular cause, company or association, the client expects him to speak up on his behalf. To do so effectively requires the ability to communicate, to articulate, clearly and concisely, the client's point of view. In order accomplish this, the lobbyist needs to be able to research, to be organized, and to put his thoughts into coherent and easily understood speech.

Well-honed research skills are essential if a lobbyist is going to have any substance to his arguments. In making a presentation, it is not enough simply to declare that a client favors or objects to the bill in question. There must be facts and figures to support the arguments that are made. To report that the proposed bill will cause an 11 percent reduction in tourism is far better than to state that the client, for example a hotel association, thinks that not as many people will visit the city. Therefore, the successful lobbyist learns where the facts are and how to get them.

Research begins by listing all possible sources of information. If there have been news stories regarding the issue at hand, these can be found at the local library. The client should present the lobbyist with all the background material at his disposal. Beyond that, the lobbyist needs to obtain copies of any legislative material that pertains to his case, such as notes of council or standing committee meetings, and/or reports submitted by investigative committees. Whenever possible he should talk to those governmental decision-makers who are involved directly. Finally, he should confer with staff people. They can be the best source of basic data, since it is their job to coordinate all the material that comes to a decision-maker or committee.

Once the facts are known, it is imperative that they be presented in an organized manner. A successful lobbyist knows how to arrange thoughts, and supporting data so that they make sense to others. His presentations are always tightly constructed. Each point flows smoothly from the one before it, and fits into a logical pattern. Presentations that ramble, that continually repeat themselves, that are vague cause deep and abiding antagonism toward the lobbyist and his client. At the very least, that type of presentation prompts a committee member, for example, to ask the lobbyist if he has anything new to add to what has already been said; a very embarrassing situation indeed. At the worst, a grossly unorganized presentation makes office holders reluctant to allow the lobbyist future access to themselves and to committee hearings. However, knowing the facts and organizing them well is still not enough to guarantee success.

A competent lobbyist must be able to present well organized supporting data in an easily understood manner. He must be cognizant of the fact that the office holders he needs to lobby may come from backgrounds quite different from his or his client's. Language, especially jargon, that is a part of the lobbyist's or his client's everyday experience may sound terribly esoteric and/or condescending to the very people he is trying to lobby. It is essential to walk that fine line between being patronizing, by being too simple, or being so technical that is sounds as though he is speaking a foreign language.

The lobbyist that begins his presentation by explaining that "the quantum theory of superannuated articulated circumlocution suggests that..." is lost before he begins. On the other hand, so is the person who begins by stating "In order to help you understand this complex bill, let me define for you some of the more difficult terms in it." The KISS theory - "Keep It Simple Stupid" - when applied to lobbying, does not mean one should insult their intelligence. It does mean, have good supporting data, organize it well and present it clearly. However, being patient, honest and easily understood may not be enough.

Sometimes, if an opposing lobbyist has all the same positive attributes, the degree of imagination brought to the presentation becomes the deciding factor. The successful lobbyist is often times the one who brings that little extra touch to his presentation. He is the one who takes mundane information and delivers it in an interesting package. It might be something as simple as using graphs or pictures. Perhaps, it means bringing people into the hearing room who will be personally affected by the legislation - not to speak, just to be seen. It could be something as quiet as presenting a bound copy of his statement to each committee member, and then speaking only in general terms, or as dramatic as arranging for a bus to take the committee to the site in question for a first hand look. In other words, the lobbyist who skillfully adds drama, or flair, to his presentation - all other things being equal - is the one the committee remembers in the more positive light.

What if an individual does not possess all these wonderful personality traits? Does that mean he can never achieve success in the lobbying field? Not necessarily. Integrity, reasonable powers of persuasion and imagination, coupled with some of the following attributes can go far toward helping someone become an effective lobbyist. Even though it is not yet possible to receive a degree in lobbying, one of the most important of these attributes is

Where do lobbyists come from? Some come from within organizations, and they know that organization well. A former lobbyist for a telephone company climbed poles, worked the lines, and repaired meters. He worked his way up. If you asked him about how the phone company does it's business, he knew. He also had that unique ability, because he did not learn in a classroom, to understand the legislative and political process.
 F. Woods, Lobbyist

education. It can be a decided asset, especially if the individual is knowledgeable in a field that is affected by public policy, and therefore, open to lobbying. For example, knowing a great deal about parking cars didn't seem particularly important in the l930's and '40's. Today, it is an $8 billion a year industry with its own national organization, as well as numerous state and local associations, many of them with their own lobbyists. The same thing can be said for such diverse fields as refuse removal, environmental concerns, private schools, and tax reform. As such, an individual who is interested in a highly specialized area such as taxation or pharmaceuticals should major in that field.

On the other hand, a person who has a general academic education finds it helpful to simply look around. By doing so, it is possible to discover an interesting field that seems to be open to lobbying Having settled on an area of specialization, the perspective lobbyist must study it thoroughly. This can be accomplished by taking a job in the field, or enrolling in classes at a local school, or simply talking to those in the business. In other words, he must decide which approach is best suited to his own personality and needs. Securing a job in the field is probably the easiest way for an individual to become a lobbyist who specializes in the concerns of that industry or group. In fact, many major corporations do not hire outside lobbyists, but rely on their own in-house personnel. Therefore, anyone wishing to specialize in lobbying for public utilities or billboard companies, to name just two such industries, needs to secure employment with one of these corporations.

Other possibilities arise from the fact that many corporations lobby as part of an industry. In these cases, it is better for the individual who wishes to lobby for the dairy industry or the oil industry to find a job within the association or enterprise that conducts the lobbying for these groups. Finally, there are corporations that occasionally lobby on an ad hoc basis. This may occur if a national corporation is competing for a contract within a particular city. If Westinghouse, for example, wishes to build a light rail system within a particular urban area, it hires self employed lobbyists who are familiar with the vicissitudes of the local government that is involved to work along side its own in-house lobbyists, who are experts in transportation.

Securing these types of contracts depends almost solely on the reputation of the lobbyist at the local level. If he has been successful in dealing with transportation issues in the past, then it is more likely that he will be asked to handle this type of assignment. Obviously those who have the specialized knowledge required for this type of lobbying effort are the first one's considered. Therefore, it is safe to say that specialized knowledge can go a long way toward mitigating the lack of some of the other traits that are seen in most successful lobbyists. So can enthusiasm and energy.

No one wants to hire a lobbyist who seems to be lackadaisical, or perpetually tired. As will be seen later, lobbying involves much more than formal presentations before policy-making groups and the time required for their preparation. Time also must be allotted to one-on-one contacts, solicitation of campaign funds on behalf of office holders, attendance at fund raising events, as well as maintaining a positive relationship with clients. This is not to say that one needs to spend 23 of every 24 hours in active lobbying. However, a spirit of enthusiasm, a delight with the challenge is certainly a plus for anyone who wishes to tackle the rigors of the lobbying profession. These attributes also help the client to feel more confident about the lobbyist's ability to handle successfully the law or policy that needs to be lobbied.

At this point, mention needs to be made of some of the physical characteristics of a successful lobbyist. Of special concern are the questions of gender, age, and appearance. While most lobbyists are men, more and more women are entering the field. For instance, approximately 15% of all lobbyists in Sacramento, California are women. That is 50% more than there were 10 years ago. In some instances, being a woman makes one more effective. Feminists may hate the idea of using their gender to score a victory, but the fact still remains that some male politicians tend to be more old fashioned, and hate to turn down a woman. This undoubtedly will change as the number of women office holder's increases as well as the number of women in the field.

However, no matter what gender an individual is, neatness counts. One need not be devastatingly handsome or a ravishing beauty to lobby victoriously, but it is essential to be carefully put together. As such, an individual's general features and clothes should work together to invite respect and appreciation. The professional lobbyist should not be bizarre or too faddish. Most politicians are quite uncomfortable when confronted with the very unusual, especially as it relates to dress, hair or makeup. It is important to remember that government institutions tend to be traditional. Rarely does one see an elected politician, male or female, wearing other than a monochromatic suit, much less sporting an untidy beard or "far out" hairstyle. They expect those they deal with on a professional level to be similarly attired.

Like beauty, age is not a barrier. While neatly dressed males may dominate the lobbying field, there is no such domination by any one age group. One of the most effective lobbyists in Washington D.C. was Congressman Claude Pepper of Florida. Congressman Pepper lobbied long and hard for his contemporaries, those over 65. On the other hand, there are many successful people who are in their early to middle twenties. The effective lobbyist remembers that it is not a question of age but a question conducting himself in a mature professional manner.

Just as age is no barrier to successful lobbying, physical disability need not be a deterrent to an individual seeking to lobby. As long as an individual possesses the necessary personality attributes, and is able to communicate clearly and effectively, being confined to a wheel chair or maneuvering on crutches should not be seen an insurmountable obstacle. With the passage of legislation in recent years, lobbied by the disabled themselves, government buildings are now accessible to everyone. Two very effective individuals come immediately to mind. The first is Joni Erikson Tada, well-known singer, painter, and advocate for the rights of the physically disadvantaged. The other individual is well known wine authority Nathan Chroman, who is also extremely effective in advocating the rights of his fellow wheel chair bound constituents. Hopefully the success of these two people encourages others who are in similar situations not to discount lobbying as a vocation or avocation.

As has been shown, there are many factors that go into making someone a successful lobbyist. Fortunately, these attributes are attainable. It may take a great deal of time, and it certainly requires a dedicated effort, but if an individual is serious about becoming a lobbyist, there is no reason why he or she should not be able to reach that goal.

How do you begin? I don't know. There is no central casting, you cannot go up there and say, and "I want to be a lobbyist." There are a thousand different ways; some come out of the political arena. Some know ex-staffers. Many are attorneys. Some are contract lobbyists, taking on any number of accounts. Some, as I say, come out of the bowels of an organization itself. They become its governmental relation's man, and do that work.

I have had many students come and say "How do you do it?" and I don't have that answer, except print up a lot of biographies and do an awful lot of walking and don't give up.

Ken Walters, Lobbyist and teacher

Chapter V - **GOVERNMENTAL PROCEDURES**

"No matter who tells you differently, it's all in the procedures. You have to know the _what_ as well as the _who_. If you don't, whatever you are trying to accomplish will never come to pass."

FEDERAL PROCEDURES

Even though all lobbyists work within the governmental structure, not all lobbyists were political science majors in school. Therefore, it is important that they have a general knowledge of how the various branches and levels of our government function, in order to have a firmer grasp of their role within those structures.

The following is a very general discussion of our governmental system. Starting with the most basic elements, it is necessary to differentiate between branches of government and levels of government. Within our system there are three branches, each with its own specific task to perform. The legislative branch is responsible for making the laws. The executive branch sees to it that the laws are carried out. Finally, the judicial branch punishes those who break the laws, and interprets laws and policies made by the other two branches. Looking at a detailed map of the United States, one can see that it is divided into fifty states, and that within each of those states are smaller areas such as counties, cities, etc. Each of those geographic areas, starting with national and going down to the local is referred to as a level, and each of those levels has its own government, composed of three branches,

Depending on the lobbyist's clients, he lobbies within one or more of these levels. Knowing this, it is important to explore each level in terms of the general procedures of its government. The national (federal) level is both the largest and most familiar to the majority of Americans. It is composed of Congress, (legislative branch) the President and his advisors,(executive branch), and the federal courts,(judicial branch). As has already been stated, it is the job of the legislative branch to make the laws, so we begin our discussion with the U.S. Congress

A proposed law is referred to as a bill. Anyone can write a bill. However, people within the executive branch write 90% of all bills. These legislative proposals are written in an attempt to carry out the President's campaign promises. As the United States became a major world power, the need to react swiftly to international events put more emphasis on the office of the President.

Modern presidents have reacted to this by becoming more vocal about the needs of the country, in regard to domestic affairs as well as foreign. With so much of the nation's legislation coming from the executive branch, the role of Congress has become more one of reacting to the President's agenda rather than establishing the nation's legislative agenda. This fact has a direct effect on the efforts of lobbyists, especially when the other party dominates the Congress. When conflict seems to be the common relationship between the President and Congress, more arguments arise about the content of bills. This conflict often encourages many different interests to attempt to have their points of view incorporated into law. The more interests there are, the more lobbyists are in evidence in Congressional offices and other localities where members can be found. However, to be successful, these lobbyists need a clear understanding of the legislative process.

Once a bill has been written, it is given to a member of Congress to be introduced. With the exception of revenue bills, which must start in the House of Representatives, a bill may be introduced in either house of Congress. At the time of its introduction, the title of the bill is read, it is given a number, and referred to one of the standing (permanent) committees in that house. It is these standing committees that have life and death power over legislation. Therefore, this is where most public lobbying takes place. Committees are organized by subject matter. For instance, the House of Representatives divides itself into 21 standing (permanent) committees, such as the Committee on Agriculture, and the Judiciary Committee. The same thing is true for the Senate. Some committees are considered to be more prestigious than others are. Members of both houses work very hard to become members of these committees. They generally accomplish this by working diligently for their own political party, since it is the parties that make committee assignments. It is important for lobbyists to realize that committee members take these assignments seriously. Because of this subject matter orientation, the members of these committees tend to become experts in their fields, and as such, the whole house generally accepts the committee's recommendation in regard to bills that come before it. When a committee receives a bill, there are a number of possible actions it can take. However, before a bill can even be considered by the committee, there is a very important hurdle it must over come - the chairperson of the committee. As the head of the committee, the chair has extensive powers.

Whether or not the committee considers a bill is the decision of the Chair. If it is considered, are public hearings scheduled? If so, who is allowed to speak? The Chair has the power to decide if it goes to a subcommittee and who serves on that subcommittee. If it goes to the whole house, he selects those on the committee who handle the floor debate All of these decisions come under the jurisdiction of this one person. Rarely does a committee dispute a decision by its Chair. Therefore, the lobbyist's efforts on behalf of a piece of legislation must often begin with this individual. Assuming a bill does get to the committee, the battle is far from over, for the committee itself has wide discretion over the fate of the bill.

The most common action is to kill the bill. The vast majority of bills never make it out of committee. Of those bills that do make it through, few do so unscathed. Let us assume that a bill is not going to be killed. Generally, the first thing the committee does is to hold a public hearing. The committee needs the input from those who will be affected by the bill. Public hearings are very important, because the members of the committee, and their staffs, do not have the time or resources necessary for full-scale research into the ramifications of each piece of legislation they are called on to consider. It is at these hearings where lobbyists make their formal presentations on behalf of their clients.

Once these hearings are ended, the committee has a number of options. Having heard the testimonies of those at the public hearing, the committee may decide to completely rewrite the bill (it then becomes known as a committee bill), and submit this bill to the full house, in lieu of the original legislation. If the bill is considered to have only a few problems, it could be amended; changed in some places rather than totally rewritten. Perhaps the bill is quite controversial. The committee can elect to send it to the whole house with no changes, but with its recommendation to pass or not to pass. Finally, if other, more pressing legislation comes up, or if the members feel a need for more input, the bill can be temporarily shelved. Whatever, the action, it should be obvious that lobbyists must do a considerable amount of work with committees and their staffs.

As is discussed elsewhere in the book, it is imperative that a lobbyist creates a good working relationship with a legislator's staff. The same is true for the staffs of the standing committees. It is the staff that first reviews the bills.

It is the staff that researches the bill, and interviews prospective witnesses before the public hearings. And, finally, the staff handles all correspondence relating to the bill. Therefore, a lobbyist who wishes to do the best for a client always makes it a point to know the staff, to be helpful in terms of research, to be visible. Granted, all this takes time, but it is an immeasurably beneficial use of his time.

A lobbyist also finds it to be to his advantage to understand thoroughly the role of the Executive Branch. Article II of the Constitution gives the executive power to the President. In other words, it is his duty to see to it that the laws are carried out; that is, that they are actually put into effect. Think of it this way. Congress passed a 65-MPH limit on all federal highways. Those who drive on those highways are aware of that limit because there are signs posted on all these highways. It was the job of the executive branch to place these signs - to carry out the law. As the scope and number of our laws have expanded, so has the President's executive power. Consequently, there have arisen two very important groups that both function as law administrators. The first group is the one with which people are most familiar, the President's Cabinet.

The Cabinet is composed of individuals who are appointed by the President with the advice and consent of the Senate. Most of these people have been political supporters of the President, and are rewarded for their loyalty by appointment to the Cabinet. Its members not only serve as advisors to the President, but each one also administers his or her own executive department. It is these departments that have been given the actual job of carrying out the law. Whenever a law is passed that is within the jurisdiction of one of these departments, it automatically becomes the responsibility of that department. To go back to the 65MPH example, it was the job of the Dept. of Transportation to make sure the signs were manufactured and put into place. As a general rule departments carry out laws as well as generate their own policy. Congress may legislate in a very general manner, and then leave the execution of the law to the relevant executive department. The details of how the law is to be put into effect become policy. This policy has the weight of law. Consequently, it can have an impact on an individual or a group that was not foreseen when the bill was before Congress. As a result, once a lobbyist has been successful in the final outcome of the bill, his work may not be over.

It may become necessary to present his client's views to managers within the relevant department, or to panels of officials who are contemplating exactly how the law should be implemented. While the executive departments may have considerable discretion in the execution of laws, there is another group that is usually classified under the umbrella of the Executive Branch, whose agencies are far more powerful. These agencies have been given quasi-legislative, quasi executive and quasi-judicial power. These powers make it possible for these agencies to not only to make their own laws, but also to carry them out, and to punish those who break them.

Beginning with the Interstate Commerce Commission in 1887, Congress has created dozens of executive agencies, commonly known as the "Alphabet Soup" agencies. Their names, or at least their initials, are familiar to most Americans. There is the above mentioned ICC, the Federal Aviation Administration (FAA), the Federal Communications Commission, FCC. and many, many others. The original purpose of these agencies was to regulate various interstate businesses. Congress would write a very broad law, establishing a general goal. In that same law, it would also create an executive agency that would be responsible for achieving that goal.

For example, Congress wanted to curb the abuses of the railroads in the late 1800's. Therefore, it wrote a law stating that goal, and creating the Interstate Commerce Commission. Through this Congressional mandate, the agency was encouraged to make policies, which are as binding as Congressional laws, carry out these policies, and punish those who violated them, effectively by-passing the federal court system.

As our society has become more diverse, so have our problems. Congress has continued to generate new agencies to handle these new problems. As such, in 1970 Congress passed the Clean Air Act, which required a reduction in air pollution. In order to achieve this reduction year, President Nixon used his power of executive order to create the Environmental Protection Agency. It's mandate was to decide how the goals set by Congress were to be met. Since that time, the powers of the EPA have expanded to include not only air pollution, but also water pollution, toxic waste dumping, and noise pollution; all the while maintaining its ability to make, carry out, and enforce its own "laws".

By giving these agencies this type of power, Congress has removed them from most of the limitations placed on other parts of our government by the checks and balances system. For instance, their decisions are not subject to presidential veto. Their members are appointed for very long terms, and are not subject to the senatorial approval process. Basically, the only two possible checks on their actions is a specific prohibition issued by Congress, or a declaration by the U. S. Supreme Court that a policy violates the Constitution. Obviously, these agencies are incredibly powerful, and need to be understood by anyone who might be impacted by their decisions.

In terms of their decision making process, these agencies often hold public hearings before formalizing a particular policy. For example, the EPA, when it wanted to put a tax on all forms of parking in Los Angeles, held public hearings in that city. The hearings were jammed. There were many lobbyists and local government officials in attendance, as well as private citizens who represented large and small businesses that would have been negatively impacted by the policy. Interestingly, there was not one person, of the over 300 that spoke, who argued in favor of the EPA position. In the end however, the agency decided to go ahead with its policy. Had Congress not acted specifically to prohibit the EPA from going through with this plan, it would have taken on the force of law, and all those who violated it would have been subject to punishment (fines) without benefit of judicial process. At that juncture, the only recourse remaining would have been a court case. In order to understand how that could happen, it is necessary to review some basic facts about our judicial structure.

Under our judicial system, the courts act as umpires. That is, they are impartial third parties that make sure the "rules of the game" are followed. Think of the courtroom as the arena, or field of play. The lawyers represent the two opposing teams. The jury makes the final decision as to who wins the game. And the judge makes sure that the lawyers conduct the trial fairly, and that the accused is given all the rights that are guaranteed in the Constitution. These courts of original jurisdiction, as they are called, have the power to hear two different types of cases: criminal and civil.

In a criminal case, a law has been broken, and a particular person has been singled out as the likely culprit. If the crime was a major one, such as murder, kidnapping or smuggling, the crime is referred to as a felony.

On the other hand, a lesser crime, such as disturbing the peace or petty theft is referred to as a misdemeanor. Punishment for a felony can involve at least a year in prison, and/or a fine of at least $1,000. Commonly a misdemeanor is punishable by a sentence of under one year, served in jail not prison, and/or a fine of less than a $l, 000. In either case, the defendant has the right to be represented by counsel, to know the charges, to face his/her accusers, and to have a public trial with a jury of his/her peers. However, not all trials are criminal. The most common court cases in America are civil.

In a civil case, no criminal charges have been brought, but there is a need for judicial action. There are several different types of civil cases. The most common is the suit for damage already inflicted. The damage can be physical, financial, emotional, or damage to one's reputation. In any of these cases, the plaintiff (the one bringing the suit) alleges that the defendant has injured the plaintiff in some way. It might be the result of a plane crash, a magazine article, faulty construction, a car accident, or a fall on city property. Other types of civil court actions include divorce cases, probates, injunctions, and name changes. In any of these cases, the court again acts as the impartial third party, weighing the facts, and making a decision as to the truth. This search for the truth is central to both types of original cases. However, the other major jurisdiction of our courts handles cases very differently.

Cases that fall under the appellate jurisdiction of the court system focus not on a search for the truth, but on an interpretation of the law. Appellate jurisdiction involves that ability and responsibility of the court to review a law in terms of its constitutionality. Under our Constitution, part of the checks and balances system grants the courts the right to nullify laws that are in opposition to the Constitution. This was done because of the very general character of some of the provisions within the Constitution, especially the Elastic Clause and the Bill of Rights. The Elastic Clause is found in Article I, Section 8, Clause 18. It allows the three branches to stretch their expressed powers (those specifically stated in the Constitution) in order to solve problems that did not exist at the time the Constitution was written. For example, Congress is given the expressed power to coin money, but as our country grew it was no longer feasible for everyone to carry large sums of coins. Therefore, Congress authorized the printing of paper money, using the Elastic Clause.

Similarly, the Bill of Rights (the first ten amendments to the Constitution) is written in quite broad terms. The First Amendment states that there can be no laws written prohibiting free speech. But, what did the writers really mean? Did they actually believe it was permissible for a person to enter a crowded theater and yell "Fire!" simply to watch the spectacle of the ensuing panic? By placing a like prohibition on laws regarding religion, was it their intention to allow anyone who wished to practice human sacrifice? As Congress and other legislative bodies have wrestled with these and similar questions, the appellate courts, especially the U.S. Supreme Court, have been called on to rule on the constitutionality of these laws.

To make such a ruling, a court does not look just at the facts of the case, or the evidence, nor does it hear testimony from the witnesses, or even the defendant. The appellate court hears arguments from lawyers for both sides, and then decides whether the law in question does or does not violate the Constitution. It is possible to appeal both criminal and civil cases, as long as the person bringing the appeal can point to a specific violation of his or her rights. The violation can be in the form of a statute or a procedure. The first could be called a violation of Substantive Due

Process, and the second a violation of Procedural Due Process. An example of each should help to clarify the difference. In l953, Rev. Brown brought suit in civil court in Topeka, Kansas, challenging a local ordinance that required his daughter to attend an all black school. Rev. Brown lost his suit. As a result, he appealed to the U.S. Supreme Court, charging that the Topeka Board of Education violated his daughter's rights under the l4th Amendment's guarantee of "equal protection of the law". As a result of his appeal, the Court declared that laws requiring racial segregation in public schools violated the U.S. Constitution.

In a similar manner, Clarence E. Gideon took his appeal to the U.S. Supreme Court. However, Gideon's appeal rested on a procedure, not a law. Gideon had been arrested for "breaking and entering with the intent to commit a felony". Thus, he was tried for committing a felony. At the beginning of his trial, Gideon asked the judge to appoint a lawyer for him, as he was a pauper, and had no money to hire one. The judge explained that it was not a regular procedure in Florida courts to appoint a free attorney for those on trial. The only exception was for defendants who were tried for capital offenses. As a result, Gideon was forced to defend himself. Consequently, he lost his case. While in prison he wrote his own appeal to the U.S. Supreme Court asserting that the trial judge's failure to appoint him an attorney was a violation of his rights under the Sixth and Fourteenth Amendments of the Constitution. In a unanimous decision, the court upheld Gideon's appeal, and mandated that all defendants who could not afford to hire a lawyer would be provided one by the court. Both of these decisions had immediate and nation-wide application. The same is true of most other decisions by the U.S. Supreme Court. Any similar law or procedure would automatically be null and void. This applies to federal laws and policies, as well as state and local laws. While the Supreme Court has changed its own precedents, there is no guarantee that it will do so. The only way to override a Supreme Court decision is to amend the Constitution. To date this has not been done, although there have been attempts to circumvent the court through the legislative process.

STATE PROCEDURES

Generally speaking the structures and procedures followed by most state governments are quite similar to those of the federal government. There are, however, two differences that need to be discussed. Until recently, only the governors of the states were granted the option of the item veto. In other words, the governor may veto specific items on an appropriations bill or in a budget. Even though Congress gave the President the same power, the U.S. Supreme Court has declared this action unconstitutional as a violation of the doctrine of Separation of Powers. Therefore, the president is once again required to veto an entire measure or none of it. In terms of lobbying, the item veto gives a lobbyist "one more chance" if there is an item to which his client is opposed. The second difference between the two levels involves the ability of the voters to participate directly in the legislative process.

There are three separate procedures that are generally discussed together, and referred to as "direct democracy". These procedures are the initiative, the referendum, and recall. All three can be very important to a lobbyist, and need, therefore, to be well understood. The initiative allows voters to place laws on the ballot for the approval or disapproval of the electorate. In this way the legislature is totally by-passed. In order to place a proposal (proposition) on the ballot, a petition must be presented to the Secretary of State for that state. This petition must contain the actual proposed law and the signatures of a certain percent of registered voters. Typically, the percentage required is 5% of the number of votes cast in the last general election. Once the signatures have been verified, the proposition is placed on the ballot for the next statewide election. If approved the measure becomes law. The governor cannot veto it, and, in most cases, it cannot be changed by the legislature. It is subject, as are all laws, to review by the appellate courts.

The voters in California have used this very important tool, for example, to place restrictions on lobbyists, to reform the state's property tax system, and to require the state legislature to spend less money on itself. The voters also defeated measures that would have instituted gun control, and prohibited homosexuals to teach in public schools. The initiative is unquestionably a powerful weapon, but it is not the only one given to the electorate.

Just as the voters are allowed to write their own laws, they are allowed to vote on bills already passed by the legislature. This is known as the referendum. Generally the process is divided into two types. Usually, the compulsory referendum requires that all amendments to the state constitution and all bond issues be placed on the ballot for voter approval.

Even though a measure, such as a bond issue for building new prisons may have passed the legislature and been signed by the governor, if the voters do not approve it, it is dead.

The only way to bring it before the voters again is to start the entire legislative process over again.

In addition to this compulsory referendum, some states allow a petition referendum. Like the initiative, this type of measure must have a petition that states the law to be voted on, and contains the requisite number of signatures. There is usually a provision that "urgency" matters and the state budget cannot be subject to the referendum process. Because state legislatures are empowered to define what is meant by an "urgency" matter; very few truly controversial measures are ever brought before the electorate. Consequently, this type of referendum has declined in usage in the last ten years. At the same time, the third process, the recall, has accelerated in usage during the same time period.

Through the recall, the electorate is allowed to vote an elected official out of office before the normal expiration of his/her term of office. As with the other two procedures, the recall requires a petition. This petition must state why the person should be recalled, and contain a number of signatures equal to a certain percentage of those who voted for that office in the last election. The percentage differs with the office, but more signatures are required for state office than for county, and more for county than for city. Once the signatures have been verified, an election date is set. Simultaneously, those who would like to be elected to that office, if the recall succeeds, endeavor to qualify themselves for the ballot. There are actually two elections on the recall ballot. First, people must vote yes or nor on the recall itself. Those who vote yes then vote for one of the candidates on the ballot to be elected to that position. If the official is recalled, the candidate with the most votes immediately assumes the office. It seems that the recall is more popular at the local than at the state level, and, of course, like the other two, is prohibited at the federal level.

These three procedures, the governor's right of item veto, and the sovereignty of the national government constitute the most profound differences between the state government and the federal. Basically, the legislative procedures, the functions of the three branches, the checks and balances system are the same. This is not true of the local governments within our country.

LOCAL GOVERNMENTS

County Procedures

It is within local governments that one finds the greatest variety of structures and processes. While they all maintain the idea of three branches, in some systems the functions of the branches are given to a single body, and in others the head of the executive branch is hired by the members of the legislative branch. For purposes of brevity the three most common systems are herewith discussed; one county and two city.

Since most counties contain a number of cities, towns, and villages, the jurisdiction of the county government generally encompasses only what is known as unincorporated territory. For people living within that territory, the county provides the same services as city governments do for those living in their jurisdiction. This has been the traditional division of power.

However, with the growth of urban related problems such as pollution and welfare payments, many county governments are finding their powers growing as the trend to consolidation grows. In other words, why have l5-20 cities trying to be responsible for a transient welfare population or attempting to deal with air or water pollution that has a county-wide impact? It is more cost effective to have one government entity responsible for the formulation and execution of policies as they relate to these types of problems. Consequently, members of county boards are no longer the anonymous people they have been in the past. They are now better known, and more political. Election time finds them waging full-blown media campaigns, and having expensive fundraisers in order to do so. Therefore, not only does their added power make them a viable political force, but also the structure of most county governments grants them immense power.

For most counties in the U.S. there is a governing board. It might be called the Board of Directors, the Board of Supervisors, or County Selectmen. The name is not that important, its power is. Generally speaking, the board is given the power to legislate; to enact county ordinances. However, because the vast majority of counties do not have a chief executive, the board also assumes that responsibility as well. There is no veto of the board's actions. It creates laws, and then it carries out the laws it has created. Like the executive agencies at the federal level, the only practical check on the board is the appellate court system.

In terms of its law making functions, the board usually divides itself into committees. The president or chairman of the board has the power to assign committee members, but, generally, he acquiesces to individual member's desires to chair or serve on specific committees, such as transportation or welfare. These committees have the same powers as congressional and state legislature committees. They can hold public hearings, amend, rewrite or kill proposed legislation. They just do it with fewer people. Once the committee finishes with a proposal, it is sent to the full board. As with other legislative bodies, the board almost always accepts the recommendation of the committee. After its passage, the new ordinance is then given to the proper department for execution, under the supervision of the board.

As with federal and state laws, violators of county ordinances are subject to criminal prosecution. This is usually handled through the state court system. Violators may be charged with either a felony or misdemeanor, depending upon which ordinance was broken. Those who are convicted of felonies are housed in the state prison system, and those convicted of misdemeanors are incarcerated in the county jail. Of course, those who are convicted are also protected by the Bill of Rights and have the right of appeal. Because cities also have the right to make and execute their own laws (ordinances), those who are accused of breaking them also have the right of appeal.

Most cities organize their government in one of two ways. The oldest structure is called the Mayor/Council system. This system imitates the national structure in that the electorate casts separate votes for the mayor, who heads the executive branch, and for the city council, which is the legislative branch. Consistent with the federal and state models, the chief executive, in this case the mayor, has the power of the budget. He/she, like the governor, also has the line item veto. This gives the mayor a tremendous amount of power over the city's government. It also makes him an essential element in any lobbying done on the city level. The council enacts the budget and the city's ordinances, and the mayor, through the various executive departments, sees to it that the laws are carried out. This form of government is still utilized in all the major cities of the United States, and many of the smaller ones. However, a different form has becomes popular in many cities with populations under a half million.

This newer form is known as the Council/Manager form of government. Under this plan, the elected city council hires a professional city manager. It is the manager's job to create the city budget and administer city programs. The presiding officer of the council is given the title of mayor, but sometimes it is a titular office only. The mayor gets to ride in parades, hand out the key to the city, and generally act as the official host. However, the mayor cannot veto legislation or unilaterally appoint department heads. Regardless of which form a city chooses, it is important to realize that a tremendous amount of very important legislation is enacted by city councils. As such, lobbying at this level is becoming more necessary and more lucrative.

As is evident by the foregoing description, the governments within the United States generate almost limitless opportunities for lobbying. As these public policy bodies become more powerful, the number of lobbying endeavors will increase tremendously, especially on the part of interest groups. Therefore, the next chapter presents important information on the cause and function of these essential components of the body politic.

Chapter VI – INTEREST GROUPS

"There's always a group somewhere trying to get something from the government. All I have to do is find one that I'm comfortable with, and show them how I can help them."

Those who lobby do so for some specific interest. It might be a corporation, a trade association or some other type of organization. Whatever form it takes, any body of people that attempts to affect public policy is classified as an interest group. As the United States has a plethora of such groups, all attempting to modify or create new public policy, it is essential to understand their dynamics.

I guess, to some extent, I can identify a few special interest groups; the oil industry, the trucking industry, minority advocacy groups, women's rights, Spanish surname organizations, and finally, we can come down to the local homeowners' association that happens to be against a freeway or against the location of a dump site.To some extent each of these can be seen as harmful to society, because they are special interest groups. They are seeking issues that they lobby for or against, seeking decisions that will be beneficial to them, rather or not these decisions benefit society as a whole.

   GilSmith: SCAG official

Looking at the question as to why these groups exist in such numbers, most authorities point to the following reasons.

As discussed in Chapter 5, the U.S. Constitution created a federal system that consists of three basic levels of government. These levels each have their own forms of government, which are divided into three branches. Under this system, Americans have many more points of access to policy makers than do those who live in nations that still use the older unitary system.

It is conceivable that a lobbying effort could begin in a city or county and be carried through all three levels before a final policy is formulated. For example, early efforts to eliminate segregation in public accommodations began at the municipal level. After the local government had made its decision, the losing side usually took the fight to the state legislature. Once again those who were in disagreement with those policies had the opportunity to access the federal level, resulting in such national laws as the Civil Rights Acts of 1964, 1968, 1988 and 1991. However, easy access to policy makers is only one of the contributing factors to the existence of hundreds, if not thousand of interest groups in the U.S.

Under current law our political parties are heavily impacted by the existence of direct primary elections. Whereas in other nations political parties control the nomination process, in the U.S. this process has been put into the hands of the candidates and the voters. The parties have no legitimate power to stop someone from running for nomination to a particular office. Therefore, they have no ability to maintain ideological integrity. It is possible to find policy makers in both major parties that can be classified as liberal, moderate or conservative. Since the parties lack philosophical cohesion, those who have a need to affect policy choose to work through interest groups rather than a specific party. The existence of direct primaries present another problem for parties, which also contributes to the growth of interest groups. Primaries presents another problem for parties, which also contributes to the growth of interest groups.

In view of the fact that the voters nominate candidates, parties are not allowed to contribute to primary elections. Therefore, candidates must seek out their own funds for these nominating races. Naturally, there is a mutual attraction between candidates and interest groups. The candidate needs money and the interest groups need access. It is easier and cheaper for a campaign to contact one lobbyist, who it is hoped will persuade his clients to buy a complete table of 8-10 at a fundraiser, than it is to contact ten separate individuals. Once the election is over, the winning candidate has a built-in coterie of supporters, the interest groups have another point of access and the political parties have little or no control over the policies promulgated by the candidate. However, as conducive to the growth of interest groups as our political system is, it is only one of the contributing factors. Another factor is our society itself.

Within the U.S. exist a people oftentimes characterized more by their differences than their commonalties. It is the existence of these cleavages, as they are called by political scientists, that has had a crucial impact on the development of interest groups. They have been formed to represent differences in traditions, cultures, race, ethnicity, religion, occupation, education, age, hobbies, and a host of other categories. A very brief list of examples could include the National Education Association, the National Rifle Association, the U.S. Chamber of Commerce, Common Cause, the National Council of Churches, the NAACP and the AARP. In addition, within out national legislature exist such groups of the Congressional Black Caucus and the Northeast-Midwest Economic Advancement Coalition.

Given the extremely complex character of our population and the type of political system that exists, the rise of interest groups was inevitable. However, this growth has not been consistent throughout our history.

In looking at the development of these groups, there are three factors that contributed to their creation. Periods of broad economic development have led to a substantial increase in lobbying activities. The 1860's saw the birth of groups representing farmers, newly formed craft unions, and fraternal organizations. In the same vein, the growth of industrialization and mechanization gave rise to groups representing manufacturers and retailers. As our economy continued to develop and become more diversified, so did the role of the government.

Consequently, many government policies have a direct cause and effect on the growth of interest groups. Those who fought the nation's wars oftentimes have special needs and concerns. Thus a need arises for groups that represent veterans and champion their health related concerns, their monetary needs, and, for some, their emotional condition. At the state level, one sees the rise of professional organizations, as state governments continue to cede to them the right to set occupational standards. In California real estate brokers, pharmacists, insurance brokers, lawyers, and accountants must all meet the requirements of their professional associations in order to be able to practice their craft. The same is true for the vast majority of the other states. This authority makes these professional organizations very attractive to candidates for raising funds, and allows the group easy access to policy makers. However, neither broad based economic and societal changes, nor an increase in government activity can totally explain the creation of interest groups.

There needs to be someone to advance the cause; an individual who has the vision to inspire others to become involved. In other words, there must be someone who performs the same functions for an interest group that an entrepreneur performs for a business. He or she must be willing to take a risk, have the ability to gather and organize resources and inspire others to get involved. Groups such as Common Cause and those founded by Ralph Nader are prime examples of the functions of political entrepreneurs. However, almost all interest groups can identify the specific person or persons responsible for shepherding their development and creating their agenda. A major factors that has spurred such individuals into action has been the redefinition of the government's basic role and subsequent phenomenal increase in its involvement in the lives of individuals.

This increase became the hallmark of the national government with the presidency of Franklin Roosevelt. During his tenure, and at his direction, the national government became an active partner in the economy. Economic problems were no longer viewed as self-correcting. Consequently, it was deemed necessary to utilize both fiscal (the government's budget) and monetary (the amount of money in circulation) policies to keep the economy in balance. With these safeguards in full operation, individuals and groups in the 1960s were ready to promote and increase in government activities in other areas.

As more individuals, who were born after the 1930's, entered the voting age population, they were quite willing to encourage government regulation in the areas of ecology, civil rights, consumer protection and women's issues. Since these younger voters only had experienced the government as a full partner and provider of the "best" solutions to the economy's ills, it was only natural; for them to turn to the government for redress of societal ills. Most authorities agree that the 1960's and 1970's marked a period of record growth in the number of interest groups, at all levels of government. The vast majority are still in existence and still attempting to influence policy. The question then arises, how do these groups attract and hold members?

Those groups that actively pursue legislative goals divide themselves into two categories. There are those organizations that represent other organizations. Employees of these corporations are not members of the interest groups. For example, instead of using in-house employees, trade associations and corporations may hire outside firms or individual lobbyists, on a full or part time basis.

While not a part of the organization, it is the lobbyist's responsibility to keep track of proposed changes in policy that might affect these clients. As a general rule, these outside lobbyists represent more than one client. However, they do not represent competing interests. The second category of interest groups operates differently.

These groups are directly supported by members, who rely on the group's own lobbyists to protect their stated concerns. Members are active in setting and implementing the goals of the organization, as well as, donating money for its maintenance and governmental activities. As such, people join these groups for one of three reasons. There are those who join simply for the companionship they enjoy with their co-members. While not active in policymaking or implementation, they are faithful in their contributions. This type of member is usually found at the local level, and can be counted on to assist in organizing and attending group activities.

Another segment of members tends primarily to join an organization for the material benefits it provides. Although these organizations may have local chapters, it is the national organization that attracts this second group. The AARP, in addition to lobbying on behalf of those 55 and older, also provides members with a full range of monetary benefits, such as life insurance, group travel, and discounts on prescription drugs. Other organizations that provide similar incentives include the National Education Association, the American Medical Association and most unions. While this type of member can be counted on to financially support the organization, it is the third type of members that often becomes the core of the group.

These individuals join an organization in order to support its goals. In other words, they are drawn to the stated purposes of a particular interest group. It might consist of only a few neighbors fighting for a stop light at a busy intersection, or attempting to change a school board policy. On the other hand, even large purposive groups, such as Common Cause, attract this type of member. For, although the organization is national in scope, individuals see themselves as those who come under the umbrella of its concerns. Or they see themselves as a rescuer, who can be more effective by working through such an organization. The types of members an interest group attracts, therefore, depends on how it functions, its ability to provide incentives and its stated goals.

However, the role of the lobbyist remains the same, no matter why people join, because the primary goal of any interest group is to affect public policy. If a lobbyist understands why individuals have joined the group he represents, it becomes easier to gain their support for a particular lobbying activity. Members looking for companionship can be counted on to help stuff envelopes. Those who joined for reasons of incentives can be persuaded to write to individual representatives. After all, if the group is not successful in its efforts, the incentives might have to be reduced. Those who actively support the goals of the organization can be counted on to help with strategy, implementation and financial needs of the campaign. Once the lobbyist has made the most effective use of those who belong to the organization, he can better utilize his skill on their behalf.

Because of our diverse society, and the many different types of governments, we have a huge number of interest groups. That is not all bad. Many of them work for the good of the people, not just for a small group, and often times those that represent a small group still benefit the majority.

Katherine Gray, College Professor

Chapter VII - BASIC LOBBYING TECHNIQUES

"Can virtually anyone lobby? Maybe. Can most people lobby? Probably. Can knowing the proper techniques help those who want or need to influence policy makers? Absolutely!"

In becoming a successful lobbyist it is essential to analyze carefully one's own previous experience, interests, and aptitudes. Choice of a particular area in which an individual desires to work should have some connection to one of these three. Certainly it is possible to develop a general practice, so to speak, but even then it is necessary to decide which areas or levels of governmental activity are best suited to the individual's experience and interest. This is true in nearly every aspect of lobbying, providing the governmental level chosen has some regulation or control over the subject matter which a lobbyist plans to represent.

Assume that an individual's particular interest and experience has been basically devoted to rural or agricultural pursuits. Few urban or big city councils are going to have a great deal to do with that subject. The state legislature on the other hand may generate major policies in regard to health and safety, water allocation and labor regulations.

For example the current Lobbyist Directory published by the State of California lists seventy groups concerned with Agriculture. Among those listed are the American Crop Protection Association, the California Bean Shipper Association, the National Reined Cow Horse Association, and the Western Fairs Association.Each of these groups is represented by at least one registered lobbyist.

Clearly, for those who wish to lobby for one of the above groups, previous work experience in farming or in raising and growing of livestock is preferable to knowledge of industrial machinery manufacturing or airplane production. However, previous experience in a given field is not absolutely essential to becoming a successful lobbyist, as the following examples illustrate.

At the local level, community planning, shopping centers and malls, pedestrian walkways, and bus routes are always critically important items on the agendas of most city councils. In addition to these concerns, parking, particularly off-street, to accommodate stores, business offices, and restaurants is an essential component of the general planning for any metropolitan or suburban domain.   While knowledge of one of these areas is an asset, an individual who can prove to be a quick study and gain such knowledge might be able to specialize in one of these fields

At the federal level, one finds a need for lobbyists in almost any area imaginable. While most lobbyists at that level work for major corporations or national associations, there are independent lobbyists, i.e. those with their own firms. Even though it is true that some former members of Congress or those who have served in the executive branch of the government, do become lobbyists, there are just as many lobbyists who have not been employed by any part of the public sector. Both types can be quite effective. Where a former member of Congress might have an edge in understanding the legislative process, those who have thoroughly studied how laws are made can be equally as successful

Whichever level is selected; all lobbyists actually have two separate functions. Their primary function is to lobby directly a specific piece of legislation or an administrative policy, endeavoring to bring about its enactment, have amendments added, or cause its defeat, as a particular client wishes. They are expected to engage in what is known as direct lobbying.

The practice of direct lobbying requires a high level of expertise on the part of the lobbyist. Everything that is done, everything that is said, could result in the enactment, amendment, or the defeat of a piece of legislation or a policy. The purpose of this chapter is to present a thorough discussion of these basic techniques. The next chapter describes in more detail the concept of indirect lobbying, in which lobbyists are charged with the duty of creating a continuing and positive relationship with members of the state legislature, city council,

Board of Supervisors, Congress or any other important governmental body.

This relationship might involve aiding a public official in any one of a number of different ways. Lobbyists have been called upon to provide background material for a speech that an office holder must present. They have been asked to actually write such speeches, and in the case of elected office holders, lobbyists are be expected to take an active part in soliciting campaign contributions from their clients. While, this is probably the least popular, and the least attractive, aspect of lobbying, it is an essential element of the lobbyist's job. The development of this type of relationship extends beyond the officer holders themselves.

Within the legislative branch of government, and within administrative departments as well, certain players are so important to a lobbyist's cause that to forget or overlook them can prove to be a grave mistake. They are the staff members who make that legislative or administrative machinery run. They are of almost equal importance as the elected or appointed official with the title.

However, a lobbyist's most direct, and oftentimes, public activity involves clearly presenting the client's point of view to the appropriate office holder.

Recently, I had occasion to talk with people from one of the educational television stations, and they were doing a series on legislative advocacy. The attitude of their special research people was not a great deal unlike that of many others. It occurred to me that there are several things that people forget about legislative advocacy, and that one of the most important things that is forgotten, and should always be remembered, is that people in public office are used to having themselves lobbied. You are not trying to persuade the next door neighbor. If you are a legislative advocate, you are trying to persuade someone holding public office or having power and that person is as used to that, as they would be to talking on the telephone.

It is a kind of sophistication that seems to escape many of the critics of legislative advocacy. That person is in tune with, provides it as part of his environment, finds it somewhat acceptable, probably would feel lonesome without it, and is able to handle it and cope with it.

Charles Port: City Clerk, City of Los Angeles

Whether the lobbyist is presenting testimony at a public hearing, or discussing the issue in a private meeting with a decision maker, there are basic steps which must be taken. First, any legislative matter must be regarded as serious, no matter how frivolous it might seem, or how much of a nuisance it presents. If someone has taken the time to write and introduce a piece of legislation, or a policy, it's an absolute certainty that it is important to someone's constituent.

If it has attracted sufficient attention to bring about a proposed ordinance, law or administrative change, then certainly it must be regarded thoughtfully by the lobbyist and the client. Therefore, it is essential for a lobbyist to know thoroughly the client's case: to know what that client wants and what he will accept should compromise become necessary. This means having all the facts and figures, which make up the reasoning behind a client's position. It means developing a close working relationship with the client.

In order to develop this type of relationship, the lobbyist must maintain contact with the client. One of the best ways to do this is through the use of what salesmen call the "service call". Every three or four weeks the lobbyist calls on the client, simply to see if the client needs assistance or to keep the client apprised of what is happening legislatively. This is done even if there is nothing germane to the client's interest under consideration at the time. In this way the lobbyist remains a part of the client's circle of essential people, so that there is a sense of trust that develops between the two of them.

Having generated this sense of trust makes the lobbyist's job much simpler when the time comes to battle for or against public policy. Since a lobbyist's first priority is to know what a client really wants; what are the specific goals that he hopes to achieve, knowing the client well expedites this part of the process. Once these goals have been established, the task of data gathering can begin.

Data gathering, in terms of where to find the information needed, varies with each project. As such, it is vitally important to know who has the best and most pertinent information. In some cases, a legislator's staff functions as the main repository, in others it might be a particular elected official. Governmental archives, libraries, and media files are also possible sources of needed data, as is the legislative record itself. Depending upon the level involved, some or all of the following should be thoroughly examined; legislature's public agendas, records of actions, and copies of reports. Becoming familiar with these sources and using them is crucial to any lobbying effort. It is the lobbyist's job to know the correct source for each case.

In addition to knowing who has the relevant data, it is also important to make sure the facts directly relate to, and support, the client's point of view. It is imperative that a lobbyist gathers all the pertinent information. This means not confining the search for material to one's own locale. The effective lobbyist looks at the experience of others who have faced the same type of possible government action.
He accepts the wisdom of learning from their successes and failures, and using those who have achieved similar goals as examples.

This in depth research allows the lobbyist to avoid simply stating that particular outcomes have been achieved. Instead, the effective lobbyist uses specific facts and figures, knowing that decision-makers are more likely to listen to someone they believe has researched and prepared, than to someone who presents them with unsupported generalities.

Along with collecting relevant data, the lobbyist must grasp the fine points of the decision making process for the governmental body that is to be the target of the lobbyist's effort. In making a direct lobbying approach it is vital to understand precisely who holds the ultimate decision making power. The lobbyist needs to find out whether it is, for example, a commission, a committee, a legislator, an administrator or staff member. One or several of these may hold the key to the final decision on the matter that is being lobbied.

The lobbyist, who has taken the time to develop personal relationships with those who are most often involved with issues that are vital to his clients, finds this decision fairly easy to make. He knows the legislators, knows what their constituencies are all about, knows what their problems are.

Having made this determination, the lobbyist must now do some vital groundwork. For example, an issue involves a local ordinance would place restrictions on the use of commercially zoned land. This proposal adversely effects his client. The lobbyist knows that the committee has more power over that bill than does the entire legislative body. He also knows that the staff of an individual legislator, as well as, the staff of the

I think one of the most important questions a lobbyist needs to answer is whether to talk to staff. Well, it differs in every office. Some staff people use their position as an opportunity to block. Their views may be a little bit different on an issue and they will not get the information, I am told, to a legislator. That does not happen in my office. I m confident that whatever is given to my staff member does get back to me just the way it was presented. I am very appreciative for those lobbyists who will spend the time to talk with a staff person. There are a number of ways that I think who you must learn, to a degree, how a legislator works. Perhaps, there are some will see lobbyists most of the time and there are some who relay on their staff people very heavily. There are some that like to talk to you on the way to committee all the time, or right outside the committee door or right down on the floor. I prefer talk with my staff person or a telephone call. A telephone call that is left in my office with a general position will receive attention. All of the calls are logged in with the name and telephone number and the subject matter and if I receive a call in my log from a lobbyist that says I am in opposition, I would like to talk with you further or I am in support, I will take a look at that and either call that person back and say thank you for your call and make some attempt, if I feel to have some extended dialogue, if I really need it, or if I'm going to say yes or no, if I have made up my mind. I may ask the staff person to-do that

Maxine Waters:Member of Congress

committee is usually given quite a bit of responsibility. The lobbying scene is changing. Lobbyists now find themselves working more with staff that with elected officials.

Before the era of full time, professional legislatures it was an easy matter to get to the legislator. However, with longer legislative sessions there has been a complimentary rise in the number of staff people employed by legislators. While the staff members cannot commit their boss to a particular position, they are in the position to present the results of their own research and their own opinions before the lobbyist has been heard.

Many legislators operate on the principle that a lobbyist is better served, especially during very busy times, by talking to a member of their staff. The assumption is that by talking to high ranking members of a legislator's staff, the lobbyist's message receives much closer attention than it would in a thirty second meeting with the legislator. On the other hand, there are staff members who see their positions as an opportunity to block ideas they oppose, or to guard their employers from individuals they have not had a chance to scrutinize. Knowing this enables a lobbyist to create an effective strategy for getting his information to the public official. For example, one particular lobbyist visited the office of a legislator, week after week, trying to get an appointment. They could never get their schedules together. On one occasion, the lobbyist went to the legislator's secretary, and told her he had the entire week free, hoping to be able to get some time with her boss. As the secretary began thumbing through the date book, he could see that the pages were blank. At the same time, she kept saying that each day was taken up with meetings. Finally, he suggested that she join he and the legislator for lunch. She booked him in for the next day.

In addition to being aware of the relationship of individual office holders to their staff, it is imperative that he finds out how much genuine responsibility is given to the committee's staff members. If the staff, for instance, sets the agendas for the committee's hearings, he should determine whether there are specific people or groups who seem always to receive favorable time slots. Knowing this enables the lobbyist to ascertain whether it is possible for him to be given a preferential time. When it comes to the committee itself, he reviews the committee's record, and talks to people who have been associated with the committee. In this way it might be possible to learn about the philosophical stands of its members. This type of information is always helpful in preparing a presentation for committee consideration.

The successful lobbyist knows that he must attend meetings of the governmental body in question, committees as well as the full body. Furthermore he must attend these meetings long before there is a need to make a presentation.. He watches the interplay between the members, in order to become aware of who gets heard and who doesn't.

He listens to the types of presentations that receive favorable attention, analyzing what they have in common. That knowledge can be used to the lobbyist's advantage. He tailors his remarks so that they have a better than average chance of being received in a positive fashion by the members. Finally, he knows how important it is to learn which member(s) of the governmental body has the most influence over the others.

Once this member has been pinpointed, the lobbyist studies his or her reactions to the various presentations that are made. In this way, he can avoid, if possible, the type of presentation that elicits a negative response. Being armed with the data, and aware of power structure within the targeted governmental body, it is possible to plan and execute the lobbyist's presentation.

Before the presentation is written, the data should be organized along the following lines. Data that relates to the actual policy or subject that is of concern to the lobbyist and the client should be placed together. It is necessary to know why the proposal was written, and to learn the points of view of others who will also be affected by it. By doing so, their assumptions can be supported or challenged.

Looking at the relevant material, the lobbyist makes an educated guess as to the types of questions he might be asked, and prepares answers to them. Knowing his own case so thoroughly, ameliorates the possibility of having to "hem and haw" during the oral testimony. It also allows the lobbyist the address the opposition's case, and prepare for it. The final part of the presentation allows the lobbyist to challenge the arguments or those who oppose his client's position.

There could be members of the committee or commission who enjoy testing lobbyists, trying to see how thoroughly they cover all the material, not just their client's views. If their questions are not answered, there probably will not be second opportunity to do so. Therefore, being able to cover one's own case and dispel the arguments of the other side is particularly effective, whether during the committee hearing or in a one-on-one meeting with a policy maker or staff member. Once the data is organized, it is time to write the formal presentation.

Actually, the formal presentation is prepared in two parts. There is a detailed, well-written paper, which is given to each member of the governmental body in question, and an outline that the lobbyist uses during oral testimony. Both of these contain the same five elements. The first part of the presentation is a brief statement by the lobbyist as to his own name and address and the name of the client he is representing in this particular matter. Next, is a statement of the agenda item that is the subject of the presentation. After that, the lobbyist presents the basic issues that are involved.

This third section serves as the means by which the lobbyist proves to the committee that he is familiar with the policy involved, and has done enough research to be able to identify his client's concerns. Realizing that draft legislation oftentimes covers many different subjects, and may include highly detailed regulations, it is especially important for the lobbyist to clarify precisely the aspects of the legislation that are of concern to his client.

The fourth element in the report presents his (i.e. the client's) point of view, using all the data that has been collected. This section is the heart of the lobbyist's written presentation and his oral testimony. It is mandatory that this section is exquisitely organized, with effective support being given to each point that is made. In the oral presentation it is not necessary to present every piece of supportive data. However, there needs to be enough of this type of data hopefully to influence in a positive manner those members of the committee who simply skim the written report, or who see only a summary of it as prepared by their own staff. In preparing this section of the report, the successful lobbyist remembers that each committee member looks at the proposal with the idea of what is in it for his constituency. He judges what the lobbyist is proposing by whether there is anything in the proposal with which he and his constituency can favorably identify.

It is in this section of the presentation that the points of those who are on the opposite side of the matter at are offered, allowing the lobbyist to, politely of course, "shoot holes" in their arguments. It also aids friendly legislators; those predisposed to the lobbyist's point of view, in their efforts to press his point of view. Finally, any desirable or acceptable alternatives to the budget, policy, or whatever is under discussion are presented. Having completed the written part of presentation, the lobbyist is now ready to work on the oral testimony.

The primary caveat for any lobbyist is to be straightforward and honest with those one seeks to influence.

Never throw that person a curve. The surest way in the world to lose trust of decision makers is to mislead, intentionally or otherwise. A lobbyist cannot take a chance on providing information that has not been personally verified for absolute accuracy. Half-truths can be just as damaging to a career as total fabrications. It is said that the fastest way to destroy a career is for a lobbyist to deceive or lie to a legislator. This is perhaps an exaggeration, but not entirely. Legislators have long memories, and they will not forget that they have been led down the "primrose path".

Legislators depend on lobbyists for technical expertise. If a lobbyist lies, or even exaggerates, and a legislator uses that lobbyist's words on the floor, and then is embarrassed by another member, who catches the lie or exaggeration, the lobbyist's credibility is nullified. Not only will the individual legislator refuse to believe that lobbyist in the future, neither will the other legislators. Even if the offending lobbyist were able to restore his own credibility, is never the same degree of trust that existed previously.

It should be emphasized that, in like manner, threats or intimidation's do little other than raise the ire of the person who is being lobbied. Making threats in regard to marshalling votes or money against an office holder may seem like an attractive

> I think the way a lobbyist represents him or herself to a legislator is very important. When you give the information, if you purposely leave out information or mislead a legislator, that is dangerous because you have to build up some kind of trust. It is very important because, for example, you will not always be able to talk with the legislator and vice versa. If you have built up some trust over the months or years, and if you can only reach that legislator via a phone call, with you position on the bill, the legislator knows you, knows you are trust worthy and believes he can accept your position. This is very important.   Gerald Johnson, Legislator

strategy. It rarely produces the desired results. Lobbyists who are tempted to try this strategy need to remember that there are other interests, with their own lobbyists, who are willing to support the legislator in question. Since the goal of lobbying is access, withholding campaign contributions, or working against the office holder's reelection is counter productive.

Equally ineffective is attempting to intimidate office holders by raising the possibility of negative publicity, generated by the lobbyist's client, and appearing in the office holder's local newspapers. In fact, the lobbyist who engages in these types of unprofessional behavior severs a relationship that could prove quite necessary the next time around.

The second rule in oral presentations is "know your audience". It is wise to remember that legislative bodies, executive agencies and committees are basically cliques. Therefore, it is imperative to know the names of the members of the group being lobbied and how to pronounce those names. It is also helpful to know something of the history of the members, so that there is nothing in the presentation that might be considered offensive. For example, it is important to know if the female members of the committee prefer the term women to ladies. In like manner, do members prefer the designation Hispanic or Latin American, Asian or Oriental, gay or homosexual? If one member is offended, they are all offended. Not only can specific words or phrases be a "turn-off"; the manner of presentation can create a negative impression.

No one enjoys listening to a monotone voice droning on and on. Just as the lobbyist must communicate clearly and effectively with clients, he must use those same skills when lobbying political decision-makers. Too often a potentially excellent report has been ruined by poor delivery. It is extremely important to speak clearly and with inflections. Also, an effective lobbyist avoids the use of "buzz words" or jargon that might not be familiar to those who are being lobbied. There are few things more guaranteed to anger a political decision-maker than to make him feel ignorant or inadequate in public. The oral presentation should always be in clear, easily understood words, that are neither ingratiating or patronizing. These attitudes, quite quickly, generate negative reactions from those he most wants to convince. Equally as damaging to the lobbyist's position is a blatant disregard for the time commitments of those officials.

It is extremely easy to irritate or even anger a legislator. Simply ramble and repeat, emphasize and reemphasize the same point that has already made, or for that matter simply parrot something which a previous witness has just said. An astute lobbyist notices that often the chairperson patiently, or sometimes not so patiently, asks a witness not to be redundant, in view of the shortage of time and the length of the agenda. A lobbyist can generate a much more positive reception by declaring that while all of the points previously made are of great importance, he has no intention of presuming upon the decision makers' time by repeating them.

After briefly stating that he is in full agreement with the statements of specific witnesses, the effective lobbyist uses the allotted time to present material that has not been covered. He emphasizes other perspectives or facts for the committee's consideration, hoping to give those who are being lobbied "food for thought". It is definitely to the advantage of the lobbyist and his client if a lawmaker suddenly becomes inspired that the position advocated by the lobbyist is something, at least partially, of the lawmaker's origination and not something pushed on him. During this time of oral presentation, there are three other simple rules that need to be followed.

A lobbyist should not be afraid to say, "I don't know." in response to a question by a committee member. No matter how well prepared one might be, there is always the possibility of being asked an unanticipated question. Too often the temptation is for the lobbyist to think that it is better to make up an answer, after all he is a pro and should know all the answers, than to admit a lack of knowledge on the particular subject. It is far better to be honest. Volunteer to find the answer, and relay it to the one who asked, even if it is two or three days after your testimony.

This accomplishes four things for the lobbyist. It demonstrates seriousness about the subject. It shows respect for the decision-maker. It provides another legitimate opportunity for contact with the member, and it enhances credibility.

Not only is honest admission of lack of knowledge vital, so are a lobbyist's facial expressions during his oral presentation. On occasion a lobbyist may be faced with a committee that jokes among itself. Neither the reason for this behavior, nor the content of the jokes is any business of the lobbyist. Even if the members of the committee laugh at a point made by the lobbyist, he does not join in. He must keep in mind that these people see themselves as a club, and he is not a member. Therefore, whatever facial expression a lobbyist might employ to show that he is also a member of that club will be resented. It is best to simply maintain a professional demeanor.

Being aware that the committee sees itself as a club, it is imperative to always speak into the microphone and to include all of the members as the presentation is being made. In like manner, if one member asks a question, include all the members in the answer. In other words, the successful lobbyist moves his head so that he speaks to the entire panel. This may sound terribly simple, but it is well to remember that public officials have well developed egos, and do not appreciate being left out of anything that they feel pertains to them or their job.

If it is valid and permitted, and if time and room space allow, the use of visual aids, charts, computer generated presentations, video or recordings can be a highly effective adjunct to a lobbyist's presentation. However, it is wise to first clear their use with the Chairman or the clerk of the committee. Like most people, office holders don't like surprises and feel that unless they have been consulted, the lobbyist may be unduly intruding on the committee's time.

Be aware that the use of such devices or equipment requires great care and advance preparation. A poorly presented presentation can do more damage than good. The effective lobbyist never takes anything for granted. Having secured permission to set up and show the material, everything is checked out in advance, as to the best place to stand, to place the screen, or chart, being especially certain that those who are most important to the lobbyist's case are most able to see. In addition it is wise to make sure that the electrical connection is made properly, lights dimmed, if necessary and that there is sufficient help. The last item on the lobbyist's checklist involves making sure that all visual aids are in their proper order. The aforementioned practice of attending committee meetings, even when there is nothing pertinent on the agenda, assists the lobbyist is being comfortable with the specifics of the room, thus making him more comfortable during his own oral presentation.

It is vital for any successful presentation that the lobbyist understands the meaning of the visual aids that are being used, so those questions, which may arise during or after the presentation, can properly be answered. All of these directions may sound elementary, but in more times than can be imagined, someone has put slides in backwards, or placed charts in incorrect order or used materials that have not been properly studied. While it may get a laugh or two, usually the laugh is on the lobbyist. The astute lobbyist keeps in mind that we have become a visually oriented society, so that whatever can be done to make a visual impact greatly enhances any presentation. Finally, he makes very sure that the visuals fit with the rest of the presentation.

As has already been discussed, all sides of any issue are presented, therefore the lobbyist remembers that the other advocates can possibly challenge everything he does or says.

The opposition can never be underestimated. One technique that can be quite effective in blunting the efforts of the opposition is the letter writing campaign. This campaign would run at the same time as the hearings, giving members even more positive input about the client's position on the issue.

Letter writing campaigns regarding your position on a bill are very effective. Many legislators, when they come to committee, bring with them a compilation of the opposition and the support. That people who support your position write letters is noted. However, it is important to be sure that there are letters from the districts or states of the members of the committees. If a member is against the lobbyist's position, and no letters in support of that position arrive from the member's constituents, his opposition will remain.

Jerry Voorhis: Member of Congress

The lobbyist can assist the client in the preparation of mailers to be sent to individuals who would be impacted by the bill. These mailers could contain instructions on what to write, and to whom, or they could include preaddressed post cards, with suggestions for a brief message. In either case, if there is a large response, it gets the legislators' attention.

However, no matter how successful this campaign is the opposition must be treated courteously and with the same respect one would like to expect from them. Rebuttals, if permitted, must be made in a polite, dignified manner. In these tense situations a lobbyist must be precise and always straight to the point.

In making a presentation to political decision makers a lobbyist may stand alone, or with allies from the industry or the firm that is being represented, or from other organizations who are seeking the same results. If these other representatives are there, they strengthen the lobbyist's position and give credence to the arguments that are presented. However, it is vital that these supporting witnesses not submit the same general information as the other presenters. It is equally important to urge them not simply to repeat the testimony that has already been given by the lobbyist.

In planning his oral presentation the lobbyist consistently needs to remind himself that his object is to create a well informed official; one who feels comfortable with the lobbyist's point of view and is willing to actively promote that position. Having finished his oral presentation, the astute lobbyist should not be in a hurry to leave the hearing room. Members of the committee may be so offended by this "eat and run" behavior, that a favorable vote could become an unfavorable one. No one should jeopardize a possible victory through thoughtless or unintentional rudeness.

Once the committee hearings are over, what is the lobbyists next step? If a vote is not taken at the hearings, the lobbyist best serves his client by maintaining regular contact with those on the committee who fully support his point of view, and with those who might be persuaded to support the client's position. Most lobbyists believe that it is a waste of time and resources to lobby those who are inalterably opposed to their position. For example, a lobbyist who is supporting a no smoking ordinance would not lobby a legislator whose main contributors are members of the tobacco industry. Yet, on each committee there are members whose position is basically neutral, in regard to the lobbyist's bill. These members may play a pivotal role in the final outcome of the committee's vote.

> Another one that I think is an important technique is to spend your first priority working the uncommitted member. You have a fairly good idea, based upon past votes, who is friendly to your side and who is not. When committees meet at the same time, same day, and different subject areas, you don't always have time to see these members, one on one, much before the hearing itself. So to narrow your scope, you go to the people that you really don't know that much about and make your case there. You can count on other people being fairly predictable. Scott Harvey, lobbyist

After all of the presentations have been made; after all of the private discussions have been held, with staff as well as with the relevant office holders, after amendments have been explored and acted upon, the legislators take a final vote. The outcome dictates the next steps a lobbyist takes. If the lobbyist's position was defeated, there may still be hope for its passage by a full committee, if the hearings were conducted by a subcommittee, or at a subsequent meeting of the governmental body involved. It is in these situations where knowledge of the rules of procedure is absolutely fundamental. Obviously it takes time to learn all of the procedures of the varying government entities that might be encountered, but without this knowledge, no lobbyist has any hope of truly succeeding.

In dealing with the legislative branch, an effective lobbyist remembers that the committee's recommendation goes a long way toward influencing a full body, such as a council, an assembly or senate, or a board of supervisors. The legislative branch places considerable faith in the judgment of the members serving on that committee and rarely overrides that decision. Therefore, the lobbyist must weigh very carefully all the evidence, all the facts that mitigate in his favor, and honestly and realistically determine whether an appeal or further fight is in the best interest of the client.

Should the decision be made to continue the effort, it is crucial that the client is aware of all factors involved. After all, it is the client who is being represented and who is paying for the lobbyist's time and expertise. If an extended effort is going to entail new expenses, such as purchasing tickets for more fund raisers, or paying for additional time and research, the decision to proceed must rest with the client. This may be the time when the lobbyist has to compromise.

Rather than being the death knell of is case, a compromise may enhance the possibility of getting all the client wants. In preparing a presentation, the lobbyist always ask for more than the client needs. This leaves the lobbyist open to compromise graciously, and still reach the client's goals. While it is smart politics not to give in too easily, it is smart lobbying not to be so stubborn that everything is lost. What cannot be won this time can always be fought for next time. However, whatever compromise is put forth, it is absolutely essential that the client be consulted before it is accepted. No lobbyist wants to be "left out to dry" should a committee accept a compromise, before being accepted by the client.

Assuming the decision to go ahead has been made, the lobbyist must ascertain which member of the committee can be persuaded to stand with him on the matter. At that point it is up to the lobbyist to convince that person, perhaps on the basis of new or insufficiently considered evidence, that there is merit in the lobbyist's position. Just as soon as it has been decided who that key person is, the lobbyist must decide on the best approach to that person, or persons if more than one can be found. What would be most likely to appeal to them? A meeting in their office at their convenience? A breakfast or luncheon meeting where the lobbyist can privately explain and explore every aspect of what he hopes to achieve with their cooperation?

> I think that as you plan your activities it will be wise to plan some early afternoon things or luncheon type events. Much of the interaction is done during the day during lunches, coffee hours, desserts or similar activities.
> John Phillips, Member of Congress

It is quite helpful to think about how serious the issue is to the legislator and to what extent he can be expected to stand up and fight on the floor for reconsideration of a formerly negative vote. The lobbyist receives more assistance from a legislator who sees the lobbyist's position as beneficial to his own constituents.

An effective lobbyist also knows the reasons behind a legislator's stand on an issue, and reflects that stand in his discussion with the legislator For example; a legislator might be opposed to a wetlands preservation bill because it will harm the farmers in his district. A lobbyist whose client also opposes the bill, but for different reasons, could open his discussion with the legislator by commenting on the harm it would do to those who already farm in the area, and then work into his clients arguments. In this way the legislator is more at ease with the lobbyist and more prone to help. The legislator also receives additional data to bolster his already existing opposition to the bill.

Assuming the lobbyist has been successful, and the original No vote has been turned into a final Yes vote, he thanks the legislator(s) who carried the fight for him in the committee. His next step is to shepherd the bill through the whole house. While the legislature usually accepts the committee's recommendation, there might be opposition from non-committee members. This is especially true if these legislators believe the bill would negatively impact their constituents. Therefore, the lobbyist maintains a positive relationship with the author of the bill and others who support his client's position. It is during consideration by the whole house that letter-writing campaigns can, again, be quite effective. If there is any doubt, once the bill has been passed, that the measure will be signed, a lobbyist contacts executive branch staff people who can help him present his client's case to the governor, etc.

On the other hand, if the full committee's vote went against the lobbyist's position, and the original No vote is sustained, the professional lobbyist keeps in mind that the same issue will probably come up again. What cannot be won this time, can be fought for next time.

There will be a next time. So, what can be done between now and then? Most importantly, the effective lobbyist stays visible. He continues to attend committee meetings, stay in touch with officials and staff members who are important to the case. It should be obvious by now that if two lobbyists speak on opposite sides of an issue, the one who is better known to the decision-makers probably receives a more favorable reception.

In addition to staying visible, keeping the client, and the case, in front of these same key people is a top priority. An effective lobbyist is always be on the alert for changes in attitudes by members of committees and/or the public that might have a positive impact on the future consideration of a client's case. During this interim time the lobbyist puts to good use the skills exercised for indirect lobbying (these skills are discussed in Chapter VIII).

Staying visible during this interim period includes the lobbyist's relationship to his client. It is important that he remains continually aware of all government decisions that might affect his client. If the client believes that everything is just fine, it is often quite difficult to garner his support for a future fight on the same subject, or if a totally new problem arises, or if it is necessary for that client to contribute to a particular official's election campaign.

Any successful lobbyist must remain cognizant of the full legislative processes that belong to the particular level and branch of government in which he is working. He can never assume that committees at the local level have the same powers as those at the state, or that the governor's powers are a complete model for those of the mayor of a particular municipality. A lobbyist also knows, at all times, the exact disposition of any ordinance, petition, or bill that could have even the remotest impact on a client. If this precaution is not followed, most likely the lobbyist, and his issue, get lost is the bureaucratic maze.

Sometimes things happen fast.   They can be proceeding with an exasperating, even excruciatingly slow pace and then all of a sudden, the move is made and the lobbyist has to be on top of it. A city council decides that taxing his client's business would be an excellent revenue generator. The council declares the bill an urgency matter and dispenses with committee hearings. The lobbyist cannot afford to wait while the client gets instructions from head quarters, or calls a board of directors meeting for a week from Tuesday. This ability to move quickly is one of the basic parts of an effective client/lobbyist relationship. The client must have faith in the lobbyist, and the lobbyist must know the client's positions so well that he can proceed without delay, when the need arises.

As he becomes more experienced the lobbyist finds that his chances of success with a motion or an ordinance are greater at the beginning of the process. The reason for this is that early on things have not yet become set in concrete. Statements have not been given out to the press or to constituencies. Office holders are not yet on record publicly and are, therefore, not as reluctant to change or alter their position. Also the lobbyist is in a better position to shape and mold, add to or delete provisions of a bill in its early stages, than after it has been subjected to the political pressures generated during committee hearings and debates.

After a committee has turned a bill or a proposed policy over to an assistant city attorney or a legislative counsel to work out certain details, it becomes more difficult to retain control. The astute lobbyist makes every effort to be consulted on the drafting of either the original measure or any amendments thereto. After the measure has been drafted, the best time to add amendments is while it is still with a committee or subcommittee. Once again, the lobbyist's relationship with committee members and their staff is of prime importance. If there is a positive reciprocity, legislators, and their staffs, are much more likely to ask the lobbyist for his solutions to a problem or suggestions on how the bill can be drawn so as to be compatible with the wishes of the client who is paying his or her fees.

It is important to note that most committees and commissions have "point members"; particularly on a citizen's commission, such as planning, recreation and parks, drug abuse, or civil rights. Members who serve at the pleasure and by appointment of the mayor, the governor or the president often look to one of the other members as the acknowledged expert in a given field. A informed lobbyist can always expect that if one member really does his homework and shows a superior working knowledge of issues before them, that certain other members invariably follow that lead. They vote with this member, secure in the knowledge that he or she has dug more deeply into the problem, and they will be safe in casting their vote as he or she does. A truly competent lobbyist always learns who that point member is, and does his best to convince that member that he has also done research on the problem, and that he can be of immeasurable help to the member and to the entire commission.

At the same time, the lobbyist realizes that he cannot ignore or dismiss the other members. Certainly not. He takes every opportunity to talk with those who may not be point members and use his ammunition well in convincing them that both their vote and their opinion are valued most highly.

If a lobbyist has developed a relationship with these other members that is based on trust, these people may seek him out. These relationships are best developed during times when the lobbyist has no matter pending before their committee or commission. Development of this relationship may involve financial support of an official's campaign, contributions to his favorite charity or dissemination of favorable publicity, or help with problems not even related to the client's interests.

This type of relationship requires that a lobbyist be available. Not only do lobbyists need access to policy makers, but policy makers need to be able to access the lobbyist. When a legislator takes the time to seek a lobbyist's opinion, there is usually a time constraint involved. As work on a piece of legislation begins to speed up, a legislator cannot wait until next week for the lobbyist to return his call. As such, the wise lobbyist is never out of touch with his office. If one is going to play, and win, in the political arena, it has to be according to the established rules of the game. However, the rewards can be well worth the effort. Rather than the lobbyist seeking an opportunity to speak, he receives an invitation to prepare arguments favoring his or her client's position and present them.

This request cannot be taken lightly. Obviously, being asked to present one's opinion is infinitely preferable to requesting time before a committee. All lobbyists hope that they become so well known and respected that not only are they sought out by citizen commissions, but also by office holders or their appointees. How the lobbyist succeeds in that interview could presage the way the matter may be decided, and his chances for being asked for his opinion on other issues in the future. Even if the request is only tangentially connected to his client's areas of concern or seems to be a waste of the lobbyist's time, the proficient individual prepares the material with care. He makes sure that the presentation is as thorough as possible, and presented in a professional manner. For, while this request seems trivial, the next request could be a matter that has a major impact on a client.

Whether a lobbyist has been asked to submit a report to a committee, or has asked the committee for time to speak during a hearing, it is vital that his identity is well established and well regarded. This can make a tremendous difference. If the lobbyist has to spend a good portion of the time allotted introducing himself and his client, it wastes valuable time; time that could have been used for making points in favor of the client's position. This just underscores how important it is for any lobbyist to be visible - to make sure he is known, as well as the organization or client he represents. However, if the lobbyist is faced with the prospect of talking to decision makers or staff people who are unfamiliar to him, the time spent on an introduction is vital. It sets the tone for the rest of the meeting. If he gives ambiguous or incomplete information about the issue or the client, the rest of the presentation will probably be received with something less than a positive attitude.

An easy method that avoids wasting time in the hearing or in meeting with an individual office holder is for the lobbyist to write or telephone one of the official's chief assistants prior to the meeting. The written material or the phone call need not be long, but it should include the lobbyist's name, the name of the client, and the subject of his presentation. If the lobbyist can also make it clear that this basic information is being presented ahead of time so as not to waste the time of the public official, the staff member appreciates it as does the decision-maker. Starting a meeting with a positive image of the lobbyist firmly fixed in the mind of the public official is added insurance towards a positive response. It is important for the lobbyist to remember that people don't like to guess. They don't appreciate being in the dark or having to pull out of someone what they want and why they want it. Once the preliminaries have been accomplished, the lobbyist can begin the present the client's concerns, suggestions, and/or commendations.

There are times when the lobbyist meets with a single decision maker. This individual might be the chair of the committee, the head of an agency, or the chief of staff for an influential commission member. Regardless of his or her position, the lobbyist realizes that this person is crucial to the success of his client's case. As is true for presentations before committees, there are a few cardinal rules that must be followed if the lobbyist is to have any hope of making a successful presentation during a private meeting. First, the lobbyist is always on time. Having to offer excuses for keeping decision-makers, or their staff, waiting can definitely work against the efforts of even the most competent lobbyist. Second, he knows with whom he is meeting. Public officials deeply resent having either their names or titles misstated or used incorrectly.

If the lobbyist was under the impression that his meeting was with a particular officeholder, and it turns out that, due to unforeseeable circumstances, he or she is asked to present the problem to an administrative aide or a deputy, the astute lobbyist makes the best of the situation, by never expressing unusual regret or disappointment. He may feel a little let down but the specific mission has not changed, and the person who has been assigned to conduct the meeting very quickly senses a second class presentation. An accomplished lobbyist remembers that this person is far closer to the actual legislator than he is and what is said to him and the impression that is made in doing so, can quite possibly be relayed to the member with even more emphasis, one way or another. A lobbyist must be flexible and creative. Therefore, he should see this as an opportunity for fine-tuning arguments and for gaining further insights into the decision-maker's thoughts about the situation. In other words, the lobbyist can capitalize upon what might seem a setback by realizing that he has been handed a real opportunity by this turn of events

However, assuming the appointment which was made results in the lobbyist meeting with the public official. The success of that meeting rests on the impression made by the lobbyist. As was said before, and it cannot be emphasized too strongly, advance homework is essential. A lobbyist must always remember that his success is built as much on the ability to gather and present data, as it is on the development of positive relationship. Once the lobbyist has the attention of the public official, it is essential to be brief but thorough. He must bear in mind that there might not be a second chance to convince this person that the case is a valid or worthy one. Second, he needs to be sure that not only is his presentation as complete as possible, answering any and all questions that may be raised, but he needs to make doubly sure that everything that is said is truthful.

Another very effective, straightforward, and helpful technique in such an interview is to try to anticipate the arguments that an opposing side might make. This, lets the decision-maker know that the lobbyist is even more acquainted with the problem or issue than originally thought and, more than that, he has some answers to those differing positions. In addition, if the lobbyist raises the questions that will undoubtedly be asked it tends to blunt the effectiveness of the opposition. In this way, by the time the opposition meets with this same decision maker, its arguments appear to be second hand. This pre-empts the opposition to some degree.

When the opposing lobbyist does seek and receive his interview, the public official is already be somewhat familiar with the arguments or points he makes. It permits the decision-maker to question the opposition more closely and to demonstrate his competence in the area under discussion.

It is important to remember that the major task of lobbying is communication; the imparting of knowledge to a political decision maker.

To impart that knowledge in such a way as to allow the office holder to appear well versed is always to the advantage of the lobbyist. Having the lobbyist present the arguments of the other side also serves to better inform the public official so that he is as effective and knowledgeable as possible. This appeals to him as it would to anyone. Hopefully, he not only respects the lobbyist more, but he may appreciate it in a more direct way when he votes. Even if he does not, it is important for the lobbyist to keep in mind that the next time he might.

However, advance preparation is not the only concern of a lobbyist who hopes for a positive reception from a decision-maker. He must also be concerned about his office manners, the general demeanor that is exhibited during the presentation. An effective lobbyist uses the same good manners that would be used in any situation that demands he make a positive impression. As such he is not loud, profane, overly jocular. He sits where the decision-maker indicates, regardless of personal preference. A nonsmoking lobbyist, if he is wise, does not display indignation or displeasure if the public official smokes in his presence. By the same token, a lobbyist who smokes, asks permission before doing so. If there are no ashtrays present, the astute lobbyist does not even ask.

Often times, public officials have a particular preference as to the site of the meeting. If it is a one-on-one discussion it might not take place at their desk. They may have occasional chairs or a sofa, facing a coffee table, and invite the lobbyist to sit opposite them. This usually indicates that they are extending to him the courtesy and hospitality of their office. The professional lobbyist accepts this arrangement without appearing to be overly impressed or too blase.

Small talk is usually limited and this is as it should be. The lobbyist may know the decision maker's aunt, uncle, next door neighbor or daughter but does not dwell on that unnecessarily. He allows the official to take the lead.
The official involved will make it quite clear if family, friends, or social acquaintances are to be included in the discussion.
One very important thing the lobbyist must remember is to watch the familiarity. The last thing a lobbyist does, privately and even more so at a public meeting, hearing or council session is to remind an office holder about the terrific time they both had together on that recent night out. This is not only extremely poor taste but boomerangs every time.

Regardless of how juvenile all of this sounds, cases have been lost because a lobbyist forgot these rudiments of polite behavior. In other words, be friendly but not familiar. This is especially important if the office holder seems hostile to the lobbyist's position. It is important to remember that the person, who sits across the room or the conference table and argues against you today, may be the person who argues for you tomorrow.

Finally, in regard to these one-on-one meetings, a lobbyist might find it useful to suggest that he is quite willing to provide the public official with executive summaries, condensed fact sheets or any other useful data. This offer can be made on the basis that the lobbyist realizes how busy the decision-maker is; how valuable his time is. If handled in a nonpatronizing manner, this type of offer often produces great benefits for the lobbyist and the client.

As important as these private meetings may be, the successful lobbyist realizes that it is not always expedient or prudent to be a "lone wolf". At times there is a responsibility to work with others who have an interest in the same issue, even though their involvement may not be as great as that of the lobbyist. The issue he espouses, hopefully, has the support of other key individuals and organizations in the community. It is to the client's advantage, as well as his own, to accept advice and help, and to work with these other individuals toward a mutual goal. This gives both the lobbyist and the client added weight with a committee or commission. It adds responsible and perfectly ethical clout to the problem of a successful outcome.

Not only does an effective lobbyist work with those who have similar interests, he seeks the support of a legislator or public official(s) who may not be directly involved in the current legislative battle. If the legislation in question has far-reaching consequences, the legislator may have to cast a vote at some future date. Here too, decision-makers tend to follow the leader, unless these individuals have been approached and properly lobbied. If the lobbyist can involve them and get their interest, let them know that he values their time and consideration, he could collect dividends which otherwise might not be attained.

Collecting dividends is the primary objective of all the techniques presented in this chapter. The lobbyist who succeeds for his client is accomplished in all these areas. However, from the point of view of political decision-makers, expertise in presenting the client's position is not enough. Because of our current political system, and its emphasis on private funding for political campaigns, lobbyists have become an integral part of candidates' fund raising activities. This is true at all levels of government. It involves professional lobbyists, as well as those who are classified as unpaid advocates. While the vast majority of those who lobby recognize the need to be involved in these activities, they are the least attractive, and the most unpopular of all the tasks that are involved in successful, ethical lobbying.

NOTE: Because the material in this chapter is fundamental to all lobbying efforts, each of the following six vignettes contains one or more common errors made by lobbyists. Working with these should strengthen one's lobbying skills.

1. "Mr. Chairman and member of the board;
   My group feels that this proposal is really shot full of holes. It sticks it to us unfairly. There is no way we could live with it. Thank you."

2. "Madam Chairperson, members of the board;
   Hey Bob, how are you? Sure had a good time last Saturday. I am Chloe Smith, and I represent the Association of Daycare Workers. We believe that your proposal to tax the daycare industry will have serious effects on the welfare of our daycare centers. Let me show you what happened in our neighboring city where that was done."

3. " I am Zack Morgan, representing XYZ Neon Lighting Co..
   Ladies and gentlemen of the council, if you proceed with this disastrous plan to regulate neon lighting, we will have no recourse but to fight you with every means at our disposal. We will fight you in the press, and in civic meetings. We will bring in union organizers, and will shut down this city. I don't think the voters will look too kindly on you after that, Do you? Thank You"

4. "Mrs. Black, as I have already stated three times, statistics indicate, within a standard deviation of 3.5 and using a quantum analysis of mean raw figures, that restaurants with more than 20 employees will be hampered in their ability to prepare their facilities for the 'slings and arrows' they will have to face in the real world.
Thank You."

5. "Well, Mr. Gonzalez, I'm just not sure, but I'd guess that maybe three out of four cities that regulate parking companies have had negative results. But, on the other hand, maybe it's only two out of four. Yes, I'm more inclined to think it is two out of four."

6. "Mr. Chairman and members of the committee,
I am Amelia Chin. I represent the animal hospitals in this state. In regard to the proposed price control law before you, everything I wanted to say has already been said.
I just want to reiterate that those who object to this law have given you all the good arguments why it should not be passed. I don't have anything else to add, except to say that all the pet hospitals are against it.
Thank You."

Chapter VIII - INDIRECT LOBBYING ACTIVITIES

**"Like it or not, those who want a politician to
listen will find themselves being courted for
campaign contributions. Basically, the system
is based on quid pro quo."**

Within the realm of lobbying, there are two ancillary activities that a lobbyist might be called on to perform. While neither of them qualify as direct lobbying, under our definition, both are essential to the success and effectiveness of any lobbyist. The first activity is one that all lobbyists face, while the second mainly applies to those who lobby at the local level.

Going the way of all inflationary items, political fundraisers today scarcely resemble the $50 or $100 per plate dinners that used to be quite prevalent. It was once considered incredibly important to attract people to what was basically a testimonial dinner. The attendees paid their respects and gave credit to a public office holder for a job well done, with the financial proceeds, after expenses, used to pay for future campaigns. This is no longer a fact of life. The typical fund raising dinner now costs between $350 to $500 at the local level, $500 to $750 at the state level and $500 to $1,000 at the federal. Given the number of elected officials in this country, these dinners generate a tremendous amount of money.

In addition, these dinners have lost their identity as tributes. Very little attention is given to having testimonial dinners per se. They are now primarily a matter of dollars and numbers. Consequently there has developed an unspoken rivalry between offices holders within the various levels and branches. They pay close attention to how many people Congressman X had at his last dinner or Councilwoman Y had at her events. They see large crowds as direct expressions of power and support. The more people an office holder can attract to one of these functions, the more authority they feel they can exercise. Secondarily, the larger the crowd, the more supporters the candidate can claim. Both of these stands probably have some merit, but what do they have to do with lobbyists?

Very simply, lobbyists are among the most important source of campaign funds for any elected official. It is much easier for an office holder to go to one lobbyist and say, " I really would appreciate it if you (i.e. your clients) would buy a table at my next dinner." than it is for that same office holder to approach 10 or 12 people on an individual basis. This puts the lobbyist in the position of having to ask his or her clients to make one more contribution. During an election year, a lobbyist might face the prospect of having to sell tickets to 10-25 different dinners for local, state, and federal candidates for both legislative and executive positions. This can become a major expense for a company or corporation that must deal with all three levels of government, such as a public utility or a national energy producer.

The question then arises, why do it? Why not just tell the candidate that there have been so many dinners already this year, that the lobbyist's clients or his company cannot make anymore contributions? The answer to that question is summed up in one word - **access**. Office holders know that lobbyists need access to them. Without access, lobbyists cannot function. Be assured access is not the same as buying votes. Most office holders are not for sale. Consequently, if two lobbyists need to see an office holder, and one has contributed to that person's political campaigns and one has not. It is not difficult to guess which

> The big one, however, is the campaign contribution. That one provides the ultimate in access. Those of us in the public sector don't have that ability. It is against the law. It is the gift of public money. But those who have that as a tool, that is the big one. You will get a quicker response, you will get a more a more friendly response, and you may get a favorable vote more often, based on that.
>
> Jack Owens, Lobbyist

lobbyist will get the first available appointment. However, the lobbyist's involvement in fund raising does not end with the purchase of tickets. The effective lobbyist uses these events to his own advantage. Part of the ego trip for most candidates lies in their ability to attract other office holders to their fundraiser. The more that attend the more presumed power and prestige the candidate has.

Lobbyists can use this fact to their own advantage. Since office holders are loath to pay for someone else's fundraiser, lobbyists often provide tickets for them. This is not done directly. Rather, the lobbyist purchases, for example, eight tickets, but only brings four or five people to the dinner. This allows the candidate's campaign committee to use the remaining tickets for those who cannot or will not pay to attend. Knowing that a particular lobbyist donated the tickets enhances his reputation with the candidate who is holding the fundraiser, and with those office holders who are in attendance.

Oftentimes these freebies do not stay for the entire evening, but simply circulate during the predinner cocktail time. It is during this time that the astute lobbyist circulates throughout the crowd, speaking to key office holders who are in attendance. This is another productive way for the lobbyist to reinforce his visibility

In essence, political fund raising becomes a two way street. Office holders need prodigious amounts of money to run for office. Lobbyists have clients that have money that can be spent on political campaigns. Lobbyists need access to office holders. Office holders control their own calendars. Therefore, those who enable office holders to gain or retain an office have an easier time gaining access to that politician's calendar. As such, it does not pay for a good lobbyist to be out of the fund raising mainstream for very long.

The successful lobbyist realizes that he might be that office holder's only source of information on his clients and their concerns. As such, even though convincing people to buy tickets to dinners, and then, attending those dinners, can be difficult at best, in order to keep the lines of communication open, this activity is an essential part of any good lobbyist's job. It may also help with the second type of indirect lobbying activity.

From time to time, either through a referral or as a request from a client, a lobbyist is asked to prepare and submit a formal application for a zone change, a variance, or some other exception to normal planning regulations. The client may want a variance allowing a non-conforming use; or some other change in any one of many, usually complicated zoning requirements, which are part of the law. The lobbyist knows that in order to prepare an application, there is much homework to be done. Zoning regulations have become so complicated that securing any type of change transcends the expertise and time resources of the average layman. In fact, the requirements have become so onerous that today there are specialists in the field who do nothing but work on zoning or planning cases. However, even those who decide not to specialize in this field find it useful to develop basic knowledge of this type of case.

First, information and instructions are available. These can be obtained from the relevant jurisdiction and, must be read carefully. Close attention should be given to each and every detail called for in the instructions. There are no shortcuts. It is essential to become familiar with the fee schedule for filing, the number of copies of plot plans required, the deadlines for each step in the process, the list of neighboring property owners, plans for the property and how the request, if granted, will be executed. In addition, a brief written statement as to why the request should be granted must be included. If the project is of such a magnitude as to require the filing of an Environmental Impact Report (EIR), the lobbyist must be prepared to deal with another set of instructions, deadlines, fees, etc.

Undoubtedly this draconian system is the reason so few companies have been able to mold the practice of this type of lobbying into a lucrative business. The expertise that they have developed enables them to cut through the maze of bureaucratic involvement and successfully cope with the procedures that are described below.

Unfortunately, zoning cases are never inexpensive. Usually, what with application fees, engineering costs, clerical expenses, to say nothing of the lobbyist's fee, its going to cost both money and time. Many top people in planning estimate a case will take nine months from start to finish. If an EIR is required, probably the time will be doubled. Few lobbying assignments are more demanding in detail and precision as one seeking a zone change or a variance thereof.

Much success in any zoning matter depends upon knowing the rules. If the lobbyist who has been retained to shepherd through this type of change does not know the rules, he must learn them, or retain someone who does. The companies mentioned earlier who specialize therein are staffed heavily with former planning department personnel who know the rules. Map plans, petitions, signatures, names and addresses of property owners or community leaders all must be gathered and made part of the file. In many cases the Instructions include only the minimal requirements. However, most lobbyists find that additional information, references, and other supporting evidence will be necessary to build a successful case.

Applications, once filed are assigned to and reviewed by planning department staff people. Ordinarily two different hearings are held. A zoning administrator may hold a hearing on the requested change in order to judge its compliance with that jurisdiction's requirements. Later, a planning commission may hold a hearing to evaluate the impact the change will have on the surrounding areas, on traffic and on the environment. After the Planning Commission has conducted its hearing, a legislative planning committee receives its recommendations. Finally the legislative body itself will schedule the matter for consideration. If the request is denied, there is within each jurisdiction a mechanism for filing an appeal. As this process can be as complex, expensive, and time consuming as the original, it is vital that the lobbyist and his client fully understand the implications of engaging in such an appeal.

Prior to any formal hearings however, it is vital that the lobbyist contacts the local legislator who represents the district in which the subject property lies. He or she usually has a great deal to say about whether or not an application is approved or denied. Consequently, the lobbyist advises that representative as to what change is contemplated, why it is necessary and how it will improve the district.

In this type of meeting, the effective lobbyist uses the same techniques he uses when lobbying a piece of legislation. The legislator in question will undoubtedly ask the lobbyist how neighboring property owners feel about the suggested change. Have they been contacted? Does he know their attitude? Who will be most vocal with respect to actively opposing it if such opposition develops into an organized effort? If so, what standing do the leaders of such opposition have in the community? How close is their property to the subject property? Would it in fact, injure or in some way depreciate the value of or deny to them the proper usage of their property? These are the types of key issues which usually come up at the hearings that are be held.

Since it is wise to be prepared to face them before the hearings begin, the lobbyist uses this meeting as an opportunity to judge the attitude of a key player. It also gives him insights into possible opposition within the community itself. After the lobbyist has met with the office holder, the actual process beings. As a rule an application goes before a planning commission or committee after a recommendation by staff has been made.

The staff may recommend to the commission that on the basis of their findings the application should be granted, or it may recommend that it be denied. In the latter case it is far more difficult to convince the planning commissioners that they should overrule staff members who have made a study, prepared a statement or report, and answered questions in considerable detail as to why a particular zone change or variance should be granted or denied. It is the major task of the lobbyist to convince them that his arguments are superior to, or more reasonable and logical than an adverse recommendation of staff or an organized effort by opposing property owners. Doing this at least allows the lobbyist to put forth his client's case, but remember that it usually goes to a second hearing.

Generally those legislators who constitute the planning committee of the local government hold this hearing. They, in turn, consider the recommendation of the Planning Commission and in the absence of strong evidence to the contrary, will sustain that recommendation. As a general courtesy, the planning committee confers with the legislator in whose district the property lies and ascertains how he or she feels. This individual may desire to testify, and if he favors the client's position, his participation should be encouraged. On the other hand there is always the possibility of public opposition; people in the community who take their time to attend hearings and express their fears or misgivings. Of necessity the lobbyist must firmly, but in a friendly manner, try to put their fears to rest and win them to his particular point of view.

Once the committee has made its decision, the question is presented to the entire legislative body. If the committee's decision has been favorable to the client and if there is no substantial public opposition, the council's action should simply mirror that of the committee, in which case, the client now has his zone change, variance or what ever. However, if the committee's decision had gone against the client, there is still one last hope. Using all of his talents and techniques, the lobbyist must now lobby the entire body on behalf of his client. Oftentimes this is easier than lobbying a committee, since the entire body has a wider perspective than the committee. While the specific goal is not to influence pending legislation, it is clear that the lobbyist will use the same basic techniques to win the variance as he uses to affect legislation.

Chapter IX - LOBBYING AND PUBLIC RELATIONS

"A good public relations campaign may be of immense benefit to a lobbying effort. However, it is imperative to remember that lobbying and public relations are not the same."

Having addressed specific talents and skills of lobbying, a further word of clarification is needed. Although lobbying is often public in nature, it is not synonymous with public relations. Lobbying is not merely gaining publicity, or producing advertising copy. It is not engaged in image management for business and professional institutions, and it does not work primarily with the public. This is not to say that the two cannot be used quite effectively together. They can.

If a client has a public relations staff, or if his in-house executives are responsible for the public relations of his company, they can work hand-in-glove with the people who are lobbying a specific law or policy, whatever level of government might be involved. Any office holder, whether a congressman or a councilman, is far happier supporting and voting for or against a specific issue, if the media in his particular area is supporting that position. While generating these stories is a function of the public relations people, their effective use becomes the responsibility of the lobbyist. So, even though the two disciplines have separate responsibilities, they are both working toward the same end, the successful accomplishment of the client's goals.

Favorable publicity, such as stories or interviews can be used to augment the lobbyist's formal presentation to a committee or agency. This type of publicity can sometimes be as rewarding as the carefully reasoned arguments he might devise. Government decision makers, elected or appointed, like to be perceived as being on the "right side". Therefore, if the lobbyist can capitalize on publicity favorable to the client's position, it will give him an edge in dealing with these decision-makers. However he needs to make very sure that the stories or interviews are based on facts. Nothing could be more devastating to his case and/or career than to base an entire lobbying effort on unsubstantiated material.

There are other ways in which the two can work together for the benefit of the client. Public relations can be a valuable tool in helping to raise public consciousness and support for a client's cause. Those in public relations are adept at influencing the public by stimulating its interests, and getting it to act on behalf of a product or idea. As opposed to the average lobbyist, they have learned the importance of symbols, shapes, colors and catchwords for developing a reaction on the part of the people. In utilizing these arts, the public relations people can play a significant supporting role for the lobbyist. This is particularly true in cases where the public might not be aware of the need for a lobbying effort. A news story about the construction of an adult book and video store close to a school could galvanize parents. The lobbyist for other stores in the area who are also opposed to the construction can use the opposition of the parents in his presentation to the city council.

However, some situations come with a built-in public reaction. Perhaps one of the classic examples is where private companies are making a charge for a public service. For example, members of the public feel they are already paying too high a price for health care. Therefore, if a government entity were to propose to raise the price on prescription drugs through the imposition of a tax, the lobbyist finds a ready response on the part of the public. It enables him to deal quickly and negatively with that proposal. The public relations people will have no problem rallying the support of the general public.

Simply publicizing the economic consequences of the tax, by pointing out the obvious fact that they, the members of the public, will have to bare the burden of the tax is often enough to engender spontaneous telegrams and letters. These could be supplemented with preprinted postcards that those who buy prescription drugs would be given and urged to mail. This type of public relations endeavor is a natural adjunct to the lobbyist's endeavors, especially if the client, for example the Gray Panthers, is against the tax. Once the officials in question have received predominantly negative responses from the voting public, the lobbyist's job has been made infinitely easier.

An example of where this marriage of lobbying and public relations was not used is New York City. In that city there is a 14% tax on every dollar that is spent by the public on parking. That means that for every dollar charged for parking, an individual must pay $1.14, the extra$.14 going directly into the city coffers. Considering the parking charges in New York City, this tax can cost the average parker over

$2.00 a day. Evidently sufficient public awareness was not created to generate the kind of opposition that would have prevented the imposition of this tax. Where public ire has been sufficiently and effectively aroused, parking taxes have been defeated each time they have been proposed.

Rallying the public in support of a client's endeavor can be applied to many different types of proposed legislation or policies. Such diverse groups as the National Rifle Association, the National Chamber of Commerce and Common Cause use this technique. It is also employed by many smaller groups that are formed to fight just one piece of legislation.

It is essential that a lobbyist make himself aware of the great potential available in the organizing and directing of existing public opinion. However, there are times when a built-in public sentiment will work against a lobbyist's best efforts. Recently a law was passed prohibiting cigarette advertisements on billboards. In spite of prodigious efforts by the industry's lobbyists, public sentiment was too strong for the legislators to ignore.

Lobbyists can also use publicity once a governmental decision has been made. If a lobbyist has represented the unpopular side of a cause, and if his efforts have been successful, he may find it necessary, or at least desirable, to enlist the aid of those in the public relations field to help inform or educate the public as to the real story behind that side of the issue. This is especially necessary in situations where the public is directly affected by the final decision of the governing body in question. An example of where this was not done effectively involves the no smoking ban passed by the city of Beverly Hills, California.

After much debate, and long hours of discussion, the City Council passed an ordinance that banned smoking in all restaurants within the city. While the question of second hand smoke and its effects on non-smokers is still being debated between the medical community and the tobacco industry, the non-smoking residents of the city were able to mount an effective lobbying campaign, and convince the city council that second hand smoke is harmful. They stressed that this was especially true in restaurants, which tend to be rather closed environments.

However, even though these residents were successful in their lobbying efforts, they failed in the public relations department. They were not able to convince smokers that eating in a smoke free environment was good for everyone, nor were they able to convince sufficient numbers of non-smokers from other cities to abandon their favorite restaurants in favor of those in Beverly Hills. As a result, the smokers and the restaurant owners were able to launch their own successful lobbying effort. They persuaded the city council to alter the ban so as to provide for separate areas for smoking and non-smoking. Had the non-smokers done more in the area of public relations, with the non-smoking public and the restaurant owners, they might have been able to save their ban.

While lobbying and public relations are not synonymous, an effective lobbyist will welcome opportunities to become involved in positive public relations campaigns. There are two specific areas where this involvement can be quite advantageous. Whenever a lobbyist has the chance to be part of a legitimate charity fundraiser, he should endeavor to do so. This is not to say that a lobbyist must, or even should, publicize every penny he gives to a worthy cause, or every act of charity he performs. It does mean that if the lobbyist has the option of soliciting funds or of making a public contribution he should exercise it. This is especially true if the funds can be presented in the name of a client, making sure, of course, that the contribution is genuine.

Depending upon the cause involved, the lobbyist can generate even more good will for a client by allowing the public to take part in the contribution, and, then, giving the public credit for doing so. For example, a chain of retail stores could place collection bottles in all of its outlets, and promise to match whatever the public donated. At the time the donation is publicly presented to the charity, e.g. the Heart Fund or the Leukemia Society, the lobbyist for the chain would thank all the members of the public for their contributions. Simultaneously, he would extol his client's generosity in matching those funds. In this way, the organization would probably receive more money than it would have without the participation of the retail chain, the public would receive some deserved recognition, and the lobbyist would generate positive feelings toward his client.

The same type of positive response can also be created by the participation of a lobbyist in social and political community affairs. Much good can result from the cooperation of a client and the local government. Working through their lobbyist, an organization or industry might agree to publicize safety information, such as what to do in case of a natural disaster. Or, as some industries, such as the milk producers, have done, circulate information about missing children. These types of activities provide a very valuable public service, at the same time, helping to promote a positive image of a lobbyist's client.

The lobbyist can also benefit his clients by personally becoming involved in non-partisan political activities. While, it is never a good idea for a lobbyist, unless he represents a political party, to be publicly active in party politics, it is quite desirable to be appointed to non-partisan "blue ribbon" committees, task forces, and other such groups that work on problems at specific levels of government. Appointment to these types of groups is considered to be an honor. Therefore, to have a lobbyist selected for membership reflects well of his clients as well as on himself.

The successful lobbyist will always be mindful of the positive effects of public relations. He will strive to use public relations to the benefit of his clients and himself. And he will never forget that the political decision-makers he lobbies are also aware of the type of image he and his clients have generated.

Chapter X -- LOBBYING FOR ASSOCIATIONS

"Lobbying on behalf of an association may be the most rewarding, or the most frustrating type of lobbying there is."

According to the *American Heritage Dictionary* an association is "an organized body of people who have some interest, activity, or purpose in common". Every lobbyist should be familiar with this concept, since the vast majority of lobbying activity takes place on behalf of associations. There are associations that represent different trades or industries, charitable endeavors, recreational pursuits, social interests, and local concerns. If there is the remotest possibility that government could impact a group of people, there is probably an association that represents it. Among those that are most familiar to the public at large are the American Medical Association, the National Chamber of Commerce, the National Council of Churches, the National Football League, the Girl Scouts of America, and the National Education Association.

All of these, and thousands of others, find it necessary to lobby the government, either on an on-going basis, or due to a one time only situation. With governments becoming more intrusive and their procedures more arcane, associations are realizing the wisdom of hiring outside lobbyists to work for their organization. In some cases these lobbyists represent just one association; it becomes their only client. Other associations opt for hiring a lobbying firm, which represents many clients. In this case, the firm assigns one of its employees to represent the association.

A lobbyist who is approached by an association for an interview must treat it as he would any other client; keeping in mind his need to be completely honest about his experience and his personal comfort level with the government entities that have the most impact on that association. However, he will experience a different type of working relationship compared to an individual who is an in-house lobbyist for a corporation. Unlike the corporate structure, an association's lobbyist usually does not have a specific supervisor. Generally there is a board of directors that is entrusted with making policy for the association. This board may be comprised of members who are oftentimes business rivals – in the case of trade or industry associations – or those who have differing agendas for the association goals. There may be different categories of members, e.g. full, associate, and auxiliary. This type of board may generate special challenges for the lobbyist, in that one of his prime responsibilities is to maintain consensus among board members. These rivalries can generate conflicts, or at least varying goals. The lobbyist may find himself cast in the role of mediator, settling internal squabbles before being able to concentrate on the current lobbying effort. If it is a non-profit association, the lobbyist may face greater pressure to raise money for the association than to keep watch over its political goals.

A further difference between representing an association rather than a specific business involves the question of compensation. While businesses pay their in-house lobbyists a set salary and absorb their related expenses, such is not the case for associations. Compensation is generally based on an hourly rate or a set monthly retainer. Some lobbyists work on a day to day basis with a minimum per month. Other situations sometimes dictate an assignment on a case basis; said assignment may last for a year or more, depending upon the complexity of the case. Expenses incurred by the lobbyist are sometimes limited to a specific amount, or are billable to the association, with receipts being required. Depending on the association, accountability for expense may be taken very seriously, or the lobbyist may be granted wide latitude. In estimating the monetary value of an account, a lobbyist needs to be realistic. It is foolish to overcharge the client. On the other hand, undervaluing one's worth can cause the client to feel as though the lobbyist is not capable of handing the account. These financial issues need to be clarified in the contract between the two parties.

This contract should also be quite specific as to duties, benefits (if any), and grounds for termination. While a lobbyist for an association does not get involved in office politics, his expertise is more open to scrutiny. An in-house lobbyist for a corporation generally is selected from within. Therefore, there is no question about his knowledge of the business and its concerns. On the other hand, a lobbyist who is hired by an association is "taken on faith". Consequently, the contractual grounds for dismissal must be quite clear, for the sake of both parties.

Ideally an association seeks to hire a lobbyist who is knowledgeable in terms of content and process. They would like him to "speak their language"; to be familiar with the technicalities of their particular business, trade, profession or charity. However, of even more import is the lobbyist's knowledge of the political process. Familiarity with the government entities that have the greatest impact on the association is essential. This means the lobbyist knows the key personnel in legislative and executive offices, and even more importantly, is regarded favorably by those he contacts. A lobbyist may have a very active record on the county or state level, while having no experience at the municipal level. Or he may have begun his career as an aide to a member of Congress, acquiring great resources at the federal level, with no experience at the other levels.

Lobbying for an association whose purposes and goals are well understood, but which functions at an unfamiliar level is a more serious problem than the opposite scenario. The members of the association know their own subject, and can enlighten an effective lobbyist, but they need a lobbyist who is familiar with the relevant political processes. The benefits inherent in hiring this type of individual start with the client, i.e. the association, gaining a more favorable identity than perhaps existed previously. Second it acquires a recognized liaison with agencies, government offices, and elected officials, all of whom may have direct or indirect impact on the association. As his experience is a definite benefit for any association, a word of caution is required at this point.

An effective lobbyist is always in demand. For independent lobbyists, it is imperative not to take on too many accounts. As with any other profession, it is possible to spread one's resources too thin. Successful lobbying is time consuming. Realizing that proposed changes in policy can drastically effect the association, each client deserves the lobbyist's best efforts. Not only does the lobbyist need to retain sufficient time for each client's case; it is imperative that one client's interest does not conflict with another's. An independent lobbyist who represents the Sierra Club would have difficulty giving effective representation to a logging company. He would lose his credibility with both clients and the office-holders he needs to lobby.

Having too many clients will, probably, not be a problem for a lobbyist who is asked to administer an association, in addition to his lobbying duties. However, he faces other challenges. Due to budget constraints many small associations consolidate these positions. As such, the lobbyist is required to schedule meetings of the association's governing body, and set its agendas. Some system for communicating with the general membership needs to be devised. The board may decide to present educational and/or social programs to the members. It is the lobbyists /administrator's responsibility to plan and execute these events. These additional responsibilities may seem daunting. In reality, however, the lobbyist utilizes his lobbying skills in different ways. Instead of organizing a presentation to a committee, he organizes an educational seminar.

Clearly communicating with an office holder is little different from communicating with the association's members. The same people skills utilized to reach an agreement on a bill are used in defusing possible conflicts between those association members who happen to be business rivals.   Finally, there is a definite advantage to the lobbyist with this type of arrangement. By working so closely with the members of the association, the lobbyist is in a position to become extremely knowledgeable about the specifics as the business, trade, etc. that is the core of the association. In so doing, he has the opportunity to become a recognized expert in the field. This expertise will mean easier access to policy-makers, the possibility of serving as an expert witness in relevant court cases, and imbue the lobbyist and the association with greater regard by those who have contact with the lobbyist.

A lobbyist who decides to devote all, or at least a majority, of his time and talents to one association achieves a sound and long-lasting relationship with key members and leaders of a particular industry. This should not be taken lightly. As the public positions of an association are released through either interviews or press releases, the tone and public image of the organization and the profession or industry it represents and thusly, every member within it are at stake. The lobbyist must regard the publicizing of these positions as one of his most basic responsibilities. It is essential that the client be presented in the best possible light. This responsibility extends itself to other business-related activities by the lobbyist.

Civic organizations that hold strong linkage to the power holders in government are a welcome adjunct to the arsenal of lobbying efforts and techniques. Anytime a lobbyist can join an organization whose purpose compliments that of the client, he should do so. For example, if the client were a business or trade association, it would be advisable to join a chamber of commerce, the Kiwanas or Rotary, a downtown club, or a university club. Those who represent eleemosynary institutions will find the above listed organizations helpful as well. The better known a lobbyist becomes the better known his client becomes. Membership in these types of organizations existing the lobbyist with a forum for presenting his client's positions on issues and on candidates for elected offices. The additional exposure will also be to the lobbyist's benefit. He becomes a more likely candidate for appointment to special task forces, ad hoc committees, and commissions; all of which will benefit both the lobbyist and his clients.

SECTION   2

The Practice of Lobbying

A factual picture of the practice of ethical lobbying
from a politician's point of view. Statements from office
holders from all three levels of government, who
experience some contact and almost daily relationship
with lobbyists as they attempt to win favor for a client's
role or position.

In Their Own Words

**Hon. Billy Mills, Judge Superior Court,
Los Angeles**

Good Morning I thought when I left the City Council to go over across the street to the courthouse, going from the position of city councilman to that of Superior Court Judge, that I would almost immediately shed myself of all the things that I have been involved in all my life in terms of politics, in terms of the inter workings of government and that sort of thing. I think by making this statement, what I am really doing is giving you good evidence of how naive I was when I thought that was at all possible.

I had not been on the court more than three minutes before I received a telephone call that was highly charged politically. It was from a Judge who was immediately interested in convincing me that I should vote for a certain ballot proposition as a member of the bench. I told him, "well judge, I'm really disappointed. I came over here from City Hall to avoid politics and the very first call I get, as a judge, is from a politician, though he be a judge, trying to convince me that I ought to vote one way or another on a certain situation." Of course the judge was a little upset with the possibility that he completely alienated me by making a wrong choice on whether he should call me or not. He did not know that I was really sort of pulling his leg and that I understood that I was not getting completely out of politics.

I have, since my assignment on the bench, had any number of occasions to call upon my very limited experience in the area of advocacy to try to win one point or another. As a matter of fact, I found it quite desirable to be in pivotal positions right where the decisions are being made so that my influence, my opinions and the opinions of those whom I represent can be maximally felt.

I now sit as a member of the executive committee, which is the policy making body of the court, and we advise presiding judges quite often. Every now and then I'm given an assignment to go around and talk to some of the other members of the executive committee, using the exact same experience that they think I utilized when I was a member of the city council.

What I would suggest to you, even though I have been away from the immediate area of politics going on five years, I have to utilize some of the skills I learned during that previous experience, almost every day of my life since then. So what I suggest to you is that some of the things that I will share with you may not be utilized as advocates, but I believe that they will also be useful to you as you matriculate as a citizen of our community.

I would suggest that as a lobbyist, an advocate or whatever term, that you not open any presentation that you make the way that I am going to open today. I am not expecting any votes out of anyone here today, so I think I can be a little libertine in my approach.

Some people refer to lobbying as being the second oldest profession in the world. I want to argue with that presumption. I think that there is extensive evidence that lobbying is quite possibly the oldest profession and I have seen several pieces of evidence of it. First, from a biblical standpoint, I think we all must recognize the kind of coaxing and persuasion that must have gone on in the Garden of Eden, regardless of whose side you take, whether to take the side of Adam or the side of Eve or the side of either or both against the serpent, or the side of the serpent against either one or both of them. There was a certain amount of serious lobbying and a certain amount of advocacy that went on there.

A little later on in history, it was Noah himself who must have persuaded all animals in excess of two per specie and even then only one sex of each specie, to make a choice. He talked those animals into missing the boat and that included some pretty fat cats, and also convinced the people, because the evidence was rather abundant, that this was clear what was to happen, that they should stay there on whatever dry land was left and drown, while some elected dudes sailed away into the sunset, without even the benefit of a public opinion poll.

I do have some historical evidence that lobbying probably comes pretty close to being the First Profession. Recently, my family and I visited Asia Minor, and we walked down a sidewalk of a guided tour in Ephesus. There was a hieroglyphic type sign in the sidewalk and the sign consisted of two footprints, one just a little step ahead of the other, normal size male type footprints, in connection with that was a female figure supine (opposite from prone position) totally without clothes, and in addition to that there was an arrow pointing to a group of scrolls and at that precise point there was a sharp left angle that the arrow took, and behind that was a little bird, and all of that was enclosed in a rectangle. The tour guide explained the sign in the following way:

The sign says, "This is to the passing persons walking down this sidewalk, and since you apparently have nothing else to do except figure out what all this graffiti is all about, there is, housing the second oldest profession in the world, an open brothel, straight ahead and across the street from the library and to make sure that you don't get lost just follow the bird in front of you.

Now that is a rather subtle suggestion as to what an individual ought to do, and that is not completely foreign to what a good lobbyist does everyday of his life and it is one of the things I want to suggest to you today is that a lobbyist needs to be just about as subtle, but you need to be as certain and successful. As I understand from the tour guide that that particular sign was in getting people to get to the brothel, which just happened to be across the street from the library. It is clear to me that without lobbying by someone, even conceding that the first profession is the oldest, it would not be the oldest and probably would still be on it's feet if someone had not convinced somebody to do something.

What I would suggest to you is that the lobbying comes first. I'm not going to solve that problem today, but I think it is extremely important that we think about that possibility.

I need to talk to you in those terms, because a posture that I always take on whatever public statement that I make is that I am talking to the best number one talkson, ichy-bon group anywhere. I need to do that in order to communicate to you my ideas, so go along with me for a moment in my presumption, without any further proof beyond what I have already given you, that lobbyists and lobbying is an important function.

I am going to have to tell you what I feel in my heart. Tell it to you in such a way that it has to be different from what some must have told you. And if you will forgive some repetition and consider it as simply emphasis of the importance of the points that I have made, I would be greatly appreciative.

Considering the importance of a lobbyist, I think we need only consider two things. One is the importance of the public's business, which I've simply seen as the purpose of government. That is, to run the people's business. Secondly, looking at how lobbyists relate to the public business and thinking further what each of these represents, among other things. The highest practical ideas, whether you are talking about democratic form of government or more precisely, and this is in no way an expression of my political preference, a republican form of government. That ideal being that people ought to be involved in the legislative process even if one or two bodies removed by necessity. Further, that lobbying has to involve providing informational input to decision and policy makers and thirdly, we have to think in terms of harmonizing several interests.

One interest is that of the individual or group to be represented. The other is the interest of the public and I like to refer to that as the common or the public good. Hopefully, we decide, all of us who hire lobbyists and those of us who aspire to be lobbyists and those of us who perform a lobbyist function even tough we might call it something else, need to arrive at the individual interest and the public interest as a result of some very, very, strict application of intelligence rules. Finally, we need to bear in mind that there is a constant threat to all of the ideals that I have just expressed above by reason of possible abuse, extravagance and neglect by all of the people involved in the process, not the least of which are lobbyists.

It is my humble opinion that the only reasonable excuse for lobbying in the first place is to convince legislative and administrative bodies and individuals to make certain public decisions and/or do the public business in a certain way. I feel further that a department or a desk, which only performs that function on a part-time basis, can be not only a wasteful effort but it can be extremely dangerous.

To me personally, lobbying has always been like eating at a table where everyone is expected to know the rules of good table manners and where one additional factor is involved. that is how your eating is being shown on monitored network television. I believe that one, when he works as a lobbyist, does best who first familiarized himself with how that function should be before he starts doing it and he does that by a number of ways, not the least of which of course is attending vital and important meetings or seminars such as this, my contribution notwithstanding. Asking other people who know. If you need information get on the phone and ask someone, ask a colleague in the lobbying field what to do if you don't know. Finally, you should always remember that details of each work experience, for example, the relevant idiosyncrasies of those persons who you are trying to convince, like legislators. One office holder that I once knew, for example, to him the ultimate threat as far as that official was concerned is to put you under oath. If you know that he has that special idiosyncrasy and he does it every time you say something that he disagrees with, you won't be so threatened that your coolness and composure will be completely destroyed thereby denuding your effectiveness in terms of your presentation. It helps to understand and recall the relevant aspects of the characters with which you deal as an advocate.

The good advocate applies a certain kind of grace which is successful but which is always unobtrusive, non-ostentatious, except of course, as far as your clients are concerned, they must always know exactly what you are doing and why. But as far as other persons who are not your clients, who are not paying you, you must not be so glorious and you must not be so much a peacock that you are signaling what you are doing all over. Don't be too proud, don't be too showy and don't be too. flashy

The good lobbyist also takes care not to offend, by making too much of his position. Sometimes a person gets very good at the business of convincing others and he gets very cocky. I'm reminded of my first experience with a lobbyist.

Some of you may not know this but the first time I ever stepped into the council chambers was when I walked it to be sworn in as a member of the city council so there was an awfully lot I did not know. Well, there were some lobbyists there who were bright enough to appreciate the fact that there was much I didn't know and one of them thought enough of my ignorance that he came into my office, a new councilman. and proceeded to make himself comfortable by walking right past my receptionist, and none of you would ever do this, sat in the city's chair across from the chair I would normally occupy, placed one of his feet on my desk, proceeded to take from his inside coat pocket the biggest cigar that I have ever seen, which certainly exaggerated his lack of stature, because by that time he was about 4'10 and weighed about 300 pounds and was 6' wide. Started to tell me a few things that he thought that I, as a new city councilman needed to know, in order to be successful in my new role.

Well, I was not too sure of many things but, I was sure that I could physically throw the guy out of my office and that's exactly what I proceeded to do.

To give you an example of the best lobbyist I've dealt with, on the opposite extreme, I think of this in terms of what would call the spontaneous lunch. As you know lobbyists make a big deal of getting elected officials in a situation where they could talk to them very calmly in an impressive atmosphere and where everything goes well, where there can be no interruptions and in a nice restaurant. I used to receive many calls from people who wanted to have lunch with me. Lunch really turned out to be a hassle. I would go to lunch and I would do what I would call eat people for lunch.

This one lobbyist, representing one of the giant utilities was unique. he would leave the council chambers with the city council, or he would leave when they adjourned for the day. He would walk straight to my office, allowing me time to get there and he would open the door, stick his head in, and say, "is the councilman busy for lunch?" Now, he was utilizing a very interesting piece of information that who had about the way I run my office, which is another thing I want you to remember, remember the idiosyncrasies of the people with whom you must work. He knows that I leave my door open between my office and my receptionist area. So he knows that if he asks if I am doing something for lunch, that I hear that. So he says, is the councilman doing anything for lunch, and the secretary says, "just a moment, let me check with the councilman" and when she says are you doing anything for lunch? Once I said no I wasn't, I went to lunch with this man and it was one of the most pleasant experiences that I can think of because the man said, "councilman, I have a practice of never talking business at lunch. This is for us to have lunch, not to talk about anything that I need on the city council." As a matter of fact, he said, "it just so happens that I am not aware that there is anything pending on the calendar that I need to talk about." That immediately relieved me and allowed me to eat my lunch and which lends credibility to the statement he has just made to me.

This was such a pleasant experience that I got to the place where I would look forward to it. I would run out of my office in the city council, sit at my desk and wait for that gentleman to stick his head in the door and say "Is the councilman doing anything or lunch today?" And I was really disappointed when he did not do it.

Let me tell you something else. The result of that kind of conduct on the part of the lobbyist was that he did not have to contact me when he had a problem. When I thought he had a problem and when I could see it developing in the wind and through the chambers, I would take the time to go to a telephone and say, "Bill, I think you've got a problem. You better get down here and take care of it." I would say that is a perfect situation that a lobbyist should want to find himself in.

Sometimes legislators will want to do certain things for reasons that you haven't the slightest idea or guess as to why they do them. When it happens to your disadvantage, then it behooves you to find out why. If these peculiarities inure to your advantage then maybe you can spend a few minutes to wet our appetite and to help your curiosity but don't dig into it too deeply.

Now a couple of very quick points. It is extremely important that a lobbyist understands the arena within which he is required to make his presentation. There are certain things that you must know about your arena. You have to understand the acoustics, you must know which microphone works and which does not. You have to understand all the equipment that you take in, making sure the slide projector has a bulb in it, you must also make sure that your slides go in right side up, not upside down.

These things are obvious but I have seen hundreds of examples of people who are supposed to know what they are doing and who blow their entire presentation by such stupid errors as putting a slide or two in upside down

One thing to remember is something I call "political fingerprints" People, for whatever reasons, develop habits and they have voting habits. I used to do this as a member of the council. I would set up in my mind a computer run of all the city council members and I could predict almost any given issue, not only what their votes would be but what their speeches would be as well. That is why about 90% of my correspondence used to be answered sitting at my desk listening to the argument of the city council members. Don't get to convince that this is always true however.

There is such a thing as unpredictability. You need to know who is predictable and in what way and who is unpredictable.

Don't ever give up on the guy that is unpredictable because even though you will never be able to predict what he is going to do, you need to touch base with him, have him tell you what he is going to do, if he will. What I'm going to suggest is that you become a mathematician. You must be able to add, subtract, and know how to count votes.

Most of your legislators look at a package to see what is in there for them. What every proposition you put together, whatever your proposal, put it together so that everybody whom you expect to vote for your point of view can see a little piece of it in there for himself.

We like to think of that in terms of some portion of his constituency that he and his constituency can favorably identify with. In putting forth your argument, I have several little rules that I would like to pass on to you. They are not too difficult to remember. 1. Be cool, but not detached. 2. Be forceful but not emotional. 3. Be friendly, but not familiar. 4. Be truthful, but by no means clairvoyant. 5. Be adaptable, but not condescending. 6. Be clear, but not dogmatic.

Another basic thing for a lobbyist to remember is what do you do when you've won. The important thing is to know when enough is enough, already. That is the most difficult thing for a successful person to understand. His ego gets so involved until he does not want to turn a victory loose and sometimes he fouls up the whole process.

Now, I like to think that a person who has made a presentation, whether individually or to a body, should behave pretty much like a person does when he is a guest at dinner. That is, should not be in a hurry to jump up after the process and rush away. To remember that rule, just remember this, never eat and run. The reason why you don't do that is because some people get so offended by your leaving after your victory that they will turn right around, make a motion to reconsider it, and take it away. So you have to come back another day and talk to them about some other way to recoup your victory.

Finally, and by way of summary, it is very clear to anyone who reads those sections of the government code to which I have already referred, that there is a growing awareness of the public regarding their government and what their government can do with, to, and for them,

As far as the future is concerned I think we should expect that the numbers that wish to maximize their effectiveness would increase in the years ahead. This simply means that there will be a greater use and not a lesser use of the services of those, in and out of government, who understand and who can manipulate the joints of our ever-expanding bureaucracies.

Although lobbying may not be in the last profession, as it might not, in all honest, have been the first, it will unquestionably be one of the most important and heavily utilized, at least until the flood next time.

In Their Own Words...

Hon. David Cunningham,
Councilman, City of Los Angeles

Thank you very much and let me say good morning to each of the seminar participants. I see a number of individuals who are certainly much wiser in the ways of lobbying than I am. I see many that have served as effective lobbyists and whose "point" sources of information have proven to be very effective in what they do.

Let me begin by saying to you that I think it is extremely important that we all understand that lobbying liaison and thrusting forward with your point of view is an important activity, because we, as members of legislative bodies, and others who have responsibility for making public policy, and making decisions regarding public policies, often to not have the time to deal with the countless issues in depth. We are forced to make decisions so there must be a great deal of reliance on those who are experts, those who have the expertise in more intricate and detailed fashion regarding either a piece of legislation or some issue requiring a public decision. We have to rely on the kind of information that is brought to us by those experts.

I'm sure that each of you knows some of the unwritten rules that those of us who serve in public office expect from one who is a lobbyist. The object of this program is to assist you on how you can become more effective in those things that you do and how you can impact public office.

As you know, public officials are extremely busy people, not because we necessarily want to be, I guess we do want to be, otherwise we wouldn't work so hard to get elected. No one says we have to get elected; we can always take another option, which is not to be in public service.

I would suggest that if I was a lobbyist, one of the first things I would do is make certain that I had an opportunity o meet and know the staff of an elected official. Know these individuals who are important in terms of policies or certain processes in his office.

I think it is wise for you always to attempt to first speak to the elected official. If you do not have that opportunity, you should attempt to try to make an appointment to sit down and discuss it with a staff member, in depth. Have a good informative session, bring the kinds of materials that you have regarding an issue; let them know what your point of view is with reference to that issue.

Some lobbyists make a serious mistake because they refuse to talk with staff, but I am sure those of you who have been around very long realize that we do rely on a staff member to do a tremendous amount of preliminary work. They accomplish a great amount of our day to day research. We become dependent upon them for their feedback and their feelings of what has been presented.

I am sure you know that one of the other rules as a lobbyist is that you should always present the pros and cons of a matter because once we allow you a position, even if we accept what you are presenting to us as a fact, we would like to know the other side. You never know what may come from right field and if you want to make the legislator much more effective in pressing your point of view, then you must definitely share with him any weaknesses of your argument or perhaps the disadvantages of the other arguments that would weigh against the side that you are pressing for.

It is wise to be candid. In all cases it would be wise for you to indicate the exact interest that you represent; problems that you have whether you see your recommendation as the bottom line or what you think is necessary or perhaps there is some possibility for compromise..

One of the worst things you can do as a lobbyist is to falsely provide information to the elected official, misrepresent the elected official or in some way attempt to be more heavy handed than is necessary.

I am sure that each of you know your approach and how you like to operate, I can only speak from the way I like to operate. I consider myself in terms of my attitude and professional bearing and background, as a problem solver.

One of the best ways to get my hackles up is for someone to come in and say to me "I just have to do something." I don't have to do anything, particularly something that I do not believe in; particularly something that I don't have information on.

Another thing that gets my hackles up is when I am threatened. That is not a good way to make a public policy, through a threat, through retribution, and all of the other things that go along with it. I think that reasonable people can indeed disagree, and I think that they can also agree to disagree and subsequently agree if you are able to present the issues and merits of your case well.

So you have to be careful, in terms of presentation of the issue, because your object is to come out with a well informed official who feels comfortable with your point of view and is willing to become active for your position. You would be counter-productive if you came in with that as your objective and you came out, after giving an individual all of the information, all the facts, and find out that he became a persuasive adversary to your point of view. So I think that is what you are going to have to be very careful to realize and understand.

I've been asked the question; "Do I lobby?" Yes, from time to time we lobby on state issues, we lobby on federal issues and on other issues that are of concern to us. We have to lobby our other council members and try to get them to see our point of view and hope they will support us in a vote.

I've always attempted to use what I like to call the "silk glove" approach. I think that you can sit down and share the information with the individual. You ask them, do they have any questions that they want to ask of you; does he clearly understand what you are presenting. Is there is any other way you could help him understand better and does he have any problems in supporting your point of view; and is he willing to share with you whether he has problems or whether those problems could be political problems, or some of those problems could be personal. Some could be problems of principles, a problem could be that he may have committed himself earlier. I think that in the case where an individual has committed himself earlier, I try to let him know that perhaps earlier he may have committed himself without knowing the full facts surrounding an issue.

I believe in giving an individual an opportunity to come to his own conclusion and his own decision. But, I think you have to think of yourself as being in an advocacy position. I think you have to think of it as a position of really sharing factual information.

I think it pays to follow up, and if you have an issue that is extremely important, you have to start early in the game and lay out your case.

Let me give you an example of a very effective means of communicating an idea and a concern. Sometime ago many you may recall the issue dealing with Occidental Petroleum Co and their drilling site. This has been before the city council for several years.

It was before the city council before I became a councilman. My predecessor had a rather negative position regarding this matter. I picked up that position simply out of our close working relationship.

I also had an opportunity as a committee member to review all of the allegations of wrong doings. Clearly, in my mind I did not see that there had been any court case of wrongdoing. I saw that there has been some stretching by all parties involved, those for, those against, those who thought it was a good thing and those who thought it was bad. And I had clearly made up my mind that it was an issue that was way out in the Pacific Palisades area and had no impact or bearing to any real degree on my district. I voted against the drilling.

A gentleman came into my office one day and he had been a friend before I came on the council and he said: " I know your mind is made up regarding Occidental Petroleum and I don't really want to change it, but I think you have to consider whether you want to really be open minded or not.' I said, " Well, I really am close-minded about it, I've got my mind made up, I'm willing to admit that." He said, "Well do me a favor, get in the car." I got in the car and he drove me through my district. He took me to three drilling sites that I never knew existed, all three of which I had been passing every morning, about 10 blocks from my home. I never knew that any one of the three was a drilling site.

He took me to speak to neighbors, my own constituents, around these sites. As a result of his very subtle, well done presentation, and actual vivid involvement, I saw the error of having a closed mind.

I was able to take a look at the facts, which were much more factual than prejudiced.

I then arrived at a decision, which was a different decision that I had made before, but I don't think that if he had not been subtle in his approach, or if he had not taken me to my district and actually showed me what was occurring right in my own neighborhood, simply what was asked for in the Pacific Palisades, I would have never changed my mind.

Now that is an example of what I think is a very sophisticated "silk glove" way of lobbying and presenting a factual case and really being able to prove that you can be effective as an advocate for a point of view and effective in the impacting of public policy.

Let me say in conclusion, that you have to learn, you need to know the parties that are involved in a decision. You should know something about their personality. You should know something about how they react in certain situations. Many of us do not take the time to develop relationships to either our adversaries or our advocates.

In Their Own Words

Hon David Roberti
Former Majority Leader, Calif. State Senate

Thank you. I am delighted to come and talk with you though I guess my recollections will be very first hand because we are really in a heavy period at the capitol, dealing with all kinds of legislation, but this subject is very interesting because lobbying never had before been considered a profession.

After looking through the national registered lobbyist book there are enough that can easily qualify as a profession. The third definition of the noun LOBBY in Webster's Unabridged dictionary:

"The persons collectively who frequent the lobbies of a legislative house to transact business with the legislators; specifically, persons not members of the legislative body who strive to influence proceedings by personal agency; a particular group of such persons also collectively practice their methods of such persons."

The definition of the verb LOBBY is to address or solicit members of a legislative body elsewhere with an attempt to influence legislation; that is to urge or procure the passage of a bill.'

I think lobbyists are an essential part of the system, but I am glad that they are not as essential as they once were in the state Senate.

Third House members, as they are called, are an essential part of the system but they should not be the governing part of the system. Lobbyists are the purveyors of information and it would be hard, let me assure you, to legislate in a vacuum. There are several thousand bills going through the legislature during a two year session. No one person could possibly be informed on the variety of subjects that these bills cover. Each of us naturally specializes in a half dozen subject areas, according to our own interests, education and constituency. We hopefully know those areas very well but we must rely on experts for technical assistance. This is where the lobbyist enters the picture. In other words, the lobbyist is there to persuade the legislator and one of his most effective techniques is to provide hard, factual data on the bill. The lobbyist who is not well informed is a lousy lobbyist. A lobbyist who can't answer our questions on the bill is an ineffective lobbyist. He may not have all the information in his head but he had better know where to find it - fast.

A lobbyist must also be available. I know this sounds simple, but not everyone has figured this out. When I need data from a lobbyist, I am not one bit interested in waiting until next week. Things sometimes happen very fast around the legislature and the chance to make an amendment or pass or kill a bill may come and go if that person is not available to help out.

The profession of lobbying is certainly not for the lazy, although many have not heard that either and they are paid a lot more than I am in order to lobby me. There are many lobbyists who write a beautiful memo to the home office but whom I would not recognize if I saw them because they don't work the legislature. The employer of this kind of lobbyist is not really getting his monies worth. Lobbying is hard, hard work, just as legislating is hard work for the conscientious person and I hope we are all conscientious.

Obviously, a lobbyist must do more than just get his point across and more than just provide information. He must somehow persuade you to his point of view. Just how is he to do that? Intelligence helps, being a nice person helps, being a representative from an organization" point of view on which I or some other legislator has a natural sympathy helps, promoting an issue which is of great interest to my own constituency helps.

I think that any lobbyist, who works hard, can build up a trust relationship with a legislator and the staff over a period of time. I know whom I can trust, I know whom I can stand to talk to without feeling ill, I know who is reliable over the long run.

I can be persuaded to vote a certain way on issues, which are not part of my own, or my staff's areas of expertise, by truthful, helpful, reliable information from a lobbyist.

One of the ways I often make up my mind and I know other legislators do also, is to rely on one of my colleagues who is an expert in a particular field. For example, if Senator Peteris of Oakland feels a certain way in the area of taxation I would be inclined to follow his lead or at least favorably consider that point of view because he is somebody in that area that I generally agree with. Sen. Rose Ann Vuich is my expert on agriculture; she is a farmer by profession, and she represents an agricultural constituency, and she brings to that whole subject technical knowledge that I would never be able to acquire. So I simply ask her. People come to me on renter legislation because those are areas that I have frequently dealt with. In short, We lobby one another.

I can't stress too strongly the word reliability. The lobbyist who lies to you is the lobbyist who has lost his credibility and he may never get it back. I don't mind disagreeing with someone, and I hope they don't mind disagreeing with me. But if they misrepresent their point of view or if they don't tell the truth, they are no longer effective. There are lobbyists whose word cannot be relied on. I just don't give credence to their information and they don't give much value to their profession as far as I'm concerned.

Another trait counter-productive in lobbyists is being overly pugnacious and obnoxious. Some people are so convinced of their cause and the justice of their cause and that their heart is pure, that they feel they must force their views on you. I don't think they are very effective.

I really admire the person who knows the subject matter inside and out with every ramification of the subject matter. If they need technical back up they have the company attorney or the company taxman or whoever else is available, on instant call.

The capitol scene is quite different than it was not so long ago. The days when a legislator need never pay for a lunch or dinner are long gone and I don't think that's all bad. Some legislators, certainly none of my personal friends, were known to see a lobbyist in a bar and tell the barmaid to add their large bill to his tab and it was very little that the lobbyist could do about it if he did not want to offend that person. But we have taken care of that hypothetical situation, or the people have, at least. No lobbyist can spend more than a small amount, at first not more than $10 a month on a legislator or members of his staff.

The employer of a lobbyist. However, is under no such restriction, providing the lobbyist does not arrange the entertainment, so if your vice president wants to come to town and take some legislators to lunch, that is all right and the lobbyist can eat at the same table and not be contaminated by our mutual presence with each other.

Lobbying is a personal matter and much of it depends a lot on what kind of person is doing the lobbying. If I like a person I will naturally be more inclined to spend more time talking with that person. Getting work done in the Capitol is often a matter of personal relationship because people are people and that is whom we are dealing with.

You can talk in shorthand to someone you know and trust and who feels the same about you and you don't have to mince words. It takes much less time for both the lobbyist and the legislator. I can work quickly and effectively with my colleagues if I have some kind of rapport with them and if we understand each other on several levels.

One mistake the lobbyist often makes is assuming that it is absolutely necessary to see me each time he has something he wants to discus. It does not work that way. I am often called to be in three or four different places at about the same time. I cannot possibly see everyone that comes by or listen to everyone's explanation of the same bill. I hire competent staff to assume part of this burden and the lobbyist is better off going over the matter with them rather than trying to catch my attention while I am flying down the hall or on my way to committee. I cannot emphasize that too much.

Sometimes when people or lobbyists hear us say that they they think that we are just trying to put them off because we really don't want to talk with them. The fact is that having to be in 10 different places at the same time, and there is no way in 30 seconds I am going to recall the conversation that I had with the lobbyist or anyone else trying to win over my opinion after 30 seconds or after the conversation is over.

Sometimes when people or lobbyists hear us say that they think that we are just trying to put them off because we really didn't want to talk with them. The fact is, that when we have to be in several places all at the same time there is no way that in 30 seconds I am going to win over my opinion after30 seconds or whenever the conversation ended. You are much better served to talk to the staff because doing that you know your opinion is going to have a hearing and concentration and it is going to be put down in a memo and is going to reach the legislator's attention at the proper moment and not at the improper moment.

I was asked when I came in to mention something about the effectiveness of women lobbyists. Unfortunately there are still too few but the ones that we do have are very effective and their faces are well known and well regarded at the Capitol.

They are like other women who are breaking into professions that have traditionally been reserved only for men. They have to prove themselves and I'm sure they have to, unfortunately, work extra hard. But the women who are lobbyists are very effective and I think the time is coming soon when there is going to a greater need -- A greater desire, and a greater number of women lobbyists....

Lobbying as a profession can be lucrative. The most highly paid make much more than the legislators that they are paid to lobby. Some of the most effective work for little or nothing but they don't generally represent an organized trade, corporation or group.

Requirements include a thorough knowledge of the subject matter. You also need a thorough knowledge of those you are lobbying. Know the person's district and where he comes from in all other ways. Then maybe you will understand why he votes the way he does when he can vote with you on a certain bill.

You need the ability to get along well with people and the ability and willingness to spend long hours waiting and waiting and waiting. You need to be able to move quickly, if need be, and often move your organization quickly with you. If you have to wait until the monthly meeting of the Board of Directors to decide an issue that has changed on the spot in committee, you are not going to very effective.

You need to be truthful. If you don't know something, find out, but don't try to fake it. Be helpful to the legislator and his staff. You may be asking me for something. But sometimes I need help too. I might need information or help with answering the mail. I might want you to respond to my needs as well and sometimes when a lobbyist does that, especially with information which might be pertinent to the subject matter he is currently dealing with, you strike up a bond of appreciation with a legislator that is very important.

I am sorry I have so little time to spend with you this morning but the session is heavy and I have to get back on the 10:50 flight. Thanks again for inviting me to your session.

In Their Own Words ---

hon. Jerry Voorhis,
former member of Congress

I am very glad to be here to take part in an experience, which should be very useful to all of us who assume the role of an advocate. I want to start by saying I think we are considering the subject of lobbying today in a rather strange atmosphere. Traditionally, Americans have been very proud of their system of government and I think it is true that when they feel something was wrong with the government, they have a tendency to pitch in and try to make it right. I am very much afraid that today a lot of people are possessed with the idea that something is inherently bad about government itself and that politicians as a whole are a bunch of questionable characters, to say the least. So, they say, and this is a very strange thing for them to say, therefore, we won't have anything to do with political life.

I say this seems strange because they should listen to Edmund Burke, the great friend of the American colonies in the British Parliament who once said that all that good people need to do to assure disaster is nothing. In other words, the more problems we think there are in government, the more active we need to be. And, if we are a patriotic citizen, that is what we will do, we won't cop out. I'm sure we all know what the reasons are why many people feel as they do.

I believe, however, that it is quite true that most politicians are honest, conscientious people. At least they are as honest and conscientious, as they are some of their constituents. So I think we need to be supportive of government and try to have as much influence on government as we can in a constructive manner. And one way in which people can have that constructive influence is through lobbying. Lobbying does not turn me off in the least. I think it is a very legitimate and proper activity and an essential one in our democratic system of government.

I think there are some that are operating in a clandestine manner, and I don't like that. The majority of them are open and proud of their work, as they should be. And some are quite unaware of the fact that they are lobbying at all. The reason I say that is because most of us, at one time or another, engage in lobbying. If you write a letter to your congressman, you are really lobbying. And many people are engaged in trying to influence the course of the government, as private citizens and they are really lobbying. It is not what most people think of when they hear the word lobbyist. Unfortunately, the operation of a few powerful organizations and some lobbyists, who have been really trying to buy votes by favors, have given the profession an undeserved bad connotation in the minds of some people.

Most lobbyists, in my judgment, are honest people, duly registered as lobbyists as required by law and operating entirely in the open with powers of persuasion as their principal and only tool.

Some people will judge a lobbyist by the causes he represents, not by his or her expertise. For example and I'll reveal one of my concerns. I think we are headed for a monopoly of sources of energy. I won't go into that but from my point of view because I fear that as much as I do, therefore I would think that a lobbyist for the energy monopoly, which I might as well say are largely the oil companies' lobbyists, may be a bad lobbyist, but he may not necessarily be a bad lobbyist, but he is from Jerry Voorhis' point of view, because I'm against what he is doing. This really is not the proper definition of a bad lobbyist.

I want to give you a little bit of my own experience. Before I do, let me say that the real problem, in my judgement, in our system of government is that some special and very powerful interests can afford highly paid lobbyists and they do. Whereas, an organization of the people, educational organizations, churches, environmental groups, peace, or what not, generally will be inclined to look upon lobbying as something that they should not do and they lately have not done nearly as much in the line of supplying good lobbyists as I think they should. Times are changing though, and more and more we are seeing lobbyists who serve the public interest as a whole, in many ways, as well as those who serve the special interests.

I think one of the keys to a better image of lobbyists is openness plus the absence of any kind of special favors. Lobbyists work in a gold fish bowl. In many ways lobbying is the citizen's best chance to influence his government. I was a member of Congress for five terms and I considered myself an elected, hired lobbyist for the people of my district, particularly those who couldn't afford to hire anyone else.

And, as you know, Congressman go before quite a few committees to testify and they are doing a lobbying job which is one of the things they are elected to do.

On the other hand, I was lobbied plenty. I was lobbied by people from the American Friends Service, by E. Raymond Wilson, one of the most respected people in Washington. I was lobbied by two kinds of people representing sugar interests. On one hand the sugar producing farmers who wanted not to have too much sugar imported and on the other hand the big sugar refiners who wanted to have a great deal of it imported.

I had a great respect for, and really got a lot of help from some lobbyists who would give me both sides of the story. When they came in I got a lot of good useful information from them..You know, a Congressman is supposed to be someone who knows next to nothing about practically everything. So, if you can get some solid information a subject, you are eager for it. The ones I really respected were those who would say, this is our story and this is what we want to accomplish, you will probably hear this on the other side and give the pros and the cons quite effectively.

The kind of lobbying that I resented was the following: A gentleman, who was president of a very large corporation came up and knocked on the door of a little old Congressman from California and wanted to give me a map. Well, it was a nice map and what would I say,? No? I don't want the darn map? So, we got a nice map for our office. I didn't think much about it but not long afterwards we were invited to dinner at a friend's house and there was this same man and his wife. His wife soon invited my wife to go shopping with her the next day. Just think that one over a little bit. He was not a registered lobbyist. He should have been. And that kind of stuff, I resented deeply.

I recognize that every group has a right to their own point of view and the right to have that view heard and I want them to and only lobbyists can do that many times.

After I was defeated for Congress by Richard Nixon, I became a lobbyist myself. I was national secretary of the Cooperative League of the United States and accepted that post because I believed in the voluntary effort of people to solve problems by their own voluntary action. And by organizing businesses that they needed to meet their needs and solve some of their economic problems. Anyway, I was glad to register as a lobbyist and I did my lobbying largely before Congressional committees, rather than lobbying individual members that I knew before. Anyway, I knew then as I know now, any effectiveness that I may have depends entirely on the trust that people had in me and whether the members of a committee or the people I went to see really knew that I was going to try to give them an honest story.

I believe that young people might very well consider a career as a lobbyist. Particularly, if they can do it in connection with something in which they deeply believe. But their services shouldn't just be for sale The good and the effective lobbyist, as I said, operates in a goldfish bowl and uses persuasion. He or she gets to know the legislators and the executives and gains their confidence by providing solid facts and evidence in support of their cause.

I think this is one of the proper roles in our system of government. I think our people should respect it. I believe it is important for us to be active in the political life of our country and lobbying has a respected and honored place in so doing.

SECTION 3

The Regulation of Lobbying.

Inclusion of excerpts from typical laws regulating lobbying on the federal, state, and city levels.

LOBBYISTS, LOBBYING AGENTS, AND LOBBYING ACTIVITIES
Act 472 of 1978
AN ACT to regulate political activity; to regulate lobbyists, lobbyist agents, and lobbying activities; to require registration of lobbyists and lobbyist agents; to require the filing of reports; to prescribe the powers and duties of the department of state; to prescribe penalties; and to repeal certain acts and parts of acts.

History: 1978, Act 472, Imd. Eff. Oct. 19, 1978 .

Popular Name: Lobby Act -MICHIGAN

© 2003 Legislative Council, State of Michigan
The People of the State of Michigan enact:
4.411 Meanings of words and phrases.

Sec. 1.

Except as otherwise defined in this act, the words and phrases defined in sections 2 to 6 have the meanings ascribed to them in those sections.

History: 1978, Act 472, Imd. Eff. Oct. 19, 1978 .

4.412 Definitions generally.

Sec. 2.

(2) "Business" means a corporation, partnership, sole proprietorship, firm, enterprise, franchise, association, organization, self-employed individual, holding company, joint stock company, receivership, trust, activity, or entity which is organized for profit or nonprofit purposes.

(4) "Compensation" means anything of monetary value received or to be received from a person, whether in the form of a fee, salary, forbearance, forgiveness, or another form of recompense.

4.413 Additional definitions.

Sec. 3.

(2) "Expenditure" means an advance, compensation for labor, honorarium, conveyance, deposit, distribution, transfer of funds, loan, payment, pledge, or subscription of money or anything of value including a contract, agreement, promise, or other obligation, whether or not legally enforceable, to make an expenditure. Expenditure does not include the payment of a membership fee otherwise reported pursuant to section 8(1)(d) or the cost of travel to visit and return from visiting a public official for the purpose of communicating with the public official.

4.414 Additional definitions.

Sec. 4.

(1) "Gift" means a payment, advance, forbearance, or the rendering or deposit of money, services, or anything of value, the value of which exceeds $25.00 in any 1-month period, unless consideration of equal or greater value is received therefor

4.415 Additional definitions.

Sec. 5.

(1) "Legislative action" means introduction, sponsorship, support, opposition, consideration, debate, vote, passage, defeat, approval, veto, delay, or an official action by an official in the executive branch or an official in the legislative branch on a bill, resolution, amendment, nomination, appointment, report, or any matter pending or proposed in a legislative committee or either house of the legislature. Legislative action does not include the representation of a person who

has been subpoenaed to appear before the legislature or an agency of the legislature

(2) "Lobbying" means communicating directly with an official in the executive branch of state government or an official in the legislative branch of state government for the purpose of influencing legislative or administrative action. Lobbying does not include the providing of technical information by a person other than a person as defined in subsection (5) or an employee of a person as defined in subsection (5) when appearing before an officially convened legislative committee or executive department hearing panel. As used in this subsection, "technical information" means empirically verifiable data provided by a person recognized as an expert in the subject area to which the information provided is related.

(3) "Influencing" means promoting, supporting, affecting, modifying, opposing or delaying by any means, including the providing of or use of information, statistics, studies, or analysis.

(4) "Lobbyist" means any of the following:

(a) A person whose expenditures for lobbying are more than $1,000.00 in value in any 12-month period.

(b) A person whose expenditures for lobbying are more than $250.00 in value in any 12-month period, if the amount is expended on lobbying a single public official.

(c) For the purpose of subdivisions (a) and (b), groups of 25 or more people shall not have their personal expenditures for food, travel, and beverage included, providing those expenditures are not reimbursed by a lobbyist or lobbyist agent.

(d) The state or a political subdivision which contracts for a lobbyist agent.

(5) "Lobbyist agent" means a person who receives compensation or reimbursement of actual expenses, or both, in a combined amount in excess of $250.00 in any 12-month period for lobbying.

(6) "Representative of the lobbyist" means any of the following:

(a) An employee of the lobbyist or lobbyist agent.

(b) For purposes of section 8(1)(b)(i) and 9(1)(b), a member of the lobbyist or employee of a member of the lobbyist, when the lobbyist is a membership organization or association, and when the lobbyist agent or an employee of the lobbyist or lobbyist agent is present during any part of the period during which the purchased food or beverage is consumed.

(c) A person who is reimbursed by the lobbyist or lobbyist agent for an expenditure, other than an expenditure for food or beverage, which was incurred for the purpose of lobbying.

(7) Lobbyist or lobbyist agent does not include:

(a) A publisher, owner, or working member of the press, radio, or television while disseminating news or editorial comment to the general public in the ordinary course of business.

(b) All elected or appointed public officials of state or local government who are acting in the course or scope of the office for no compensation, other than that provided by law for the office. .

(8) "Mass mailing" means not less than 1,000 pieces of substantially similar material mailed within a 7-day period.

(9) "Official in the executive branch" means the governor, lieutenant governor, secretary of state, attorney general; or an individual who is in the executive branch of state government and not under civil service; a classified director, chief deputy director, or deputy director of a state department. This includes an individual who is elected or appointed and has not yet taken, or an individual who is nominated for

appointment to, any of the offices or agencies enumerated in this subsection. An official in the executive branch does not include a person serving in a clerical, nonpolicy-making, or nonadministrative capacity

(10) "Official in the legislative branch" means a member of the legislature, the auditor general, the deputy auditor general, an employee of the consumer's council, the director of the legislative retirement system, or any other employee of the legislature other than an individual employed by the state in a clerical or nonpolicy-making capacity.

(11) "Governmental body" means any state legislative or governing body, including a board, commission, committee, subcommittee, authority, or council, which is empowered by state constitution, statute, or rule to exercise governmental or proprietary authority or perform a governmental or proprietary function, or a lessee thereof performing an essential public purpose and function under the lease agreement.

4.416   Additional   definitions.

Sec. 6.

(1) "Person" means a business, individual, proprietorship, firm, partnership, joint venture, syndicate, business trust, labor organization, company, corporation, association, committee, or any other organization or group of persons acting jointly, including a state agency or a political subdivision of the state.

(4) "Local government" means a city, village, township, county, school district, or community college district.

4.416a Resignation from office; lobbying during remainder of term; violation as misdemeanor; penalty.

Sec. 6a.

(1) A member of the Michigan senate or house of representatives who resigns from office shall not make expenditures for or receive compensation or reimbursement for actual expenses for lobbying for the remainder of the term of office from which the person resigned.

(2) A person who violates this section is guilty of a misdemeanor punishable by a fine of not more than $1,000.00 or by imprisonment for not more than 90 days, or both.

4.417 Registration forms; filing; contents; failure to register; late registration fee; penalty; notice of termination.

Sec. 7.

(1) Not later than 15 days after becoming a lobbyist, a lobbyist shall file a registration form with the secretary of state.

(2) Not later than 3 days after becoming a lobbyist agent, a lobbyist agent shall file a registration form with the secretary of state.

(3) A person who fails to register under subsection (1) or (2), shall pay a late registration fee of $10.00 for each day the person remains not registered in violation of subsection (1) or (2), not to exceed $300.00. A person who is in violation by failing to register as required by this section more than 30 days is guilty of a misdemeanor, and shall be fined not more than $1,000.00.

(4) A lobbyist shall file a notice of termination with the secretary of state within 30 days after ceasing lobbying, but this will not relieve the lobbyist of the reporting requirements of this section for that reporting period. A lobbyist agent shall file a notice of termination with the secretary of state within 30 days after ceasing to lobby for a lobbyist.

4.418 Signed report; filing; form; extension; filing amended report; contents of report; reporting expenditures for food and beverage; failure to report; late filing fee; penalty; reporting activities of employee lobbyist agent; report to elected public official; preservation and destruction of statements and reports.

Sec. 8.

(1) A lobbyist or a lobbyist agent shall file a signed report in a form prescribed by the secretary of state under this section. A report shall be filed on January 31 covering the calendar year ending on the immediately preceding December 31, and on August 31 covering the immediately preceding December 31 to July 31. A report shall be filed by a lobbyist or for the lobbyist by the lobbyist agent who acts on behalf of the lobbyist, and the lobbyist agent who acts on his or her own behalf. A lobbyist or a lobbyist agent may request from the secretary of state an extension of the deadline for filing the report for a period not to exceed 60 days. The secretary of state shall respond in writing to the request, either approving or disapproving the request, and if approval is granted, the period of the extension, not later than 9 days after receipt of the request. A lobbyist or lobbyist agent may file an amended report within 1 year after the date the report is required to be filed, including an extension period.

(2) Expenditures for food and beverage provided a public official shall be reported if the expenditures for that public official exceed $25.00 in any month covered by the report or $150.00 during that calendar year from January 1 through the month covered by the report. The report shall include the name and title or office of the public official and the expenditures on that public official for the months covered by the report and for the year. If more than 1 public official is provided food and beverage and a single check is rendered, the report may reflect the average amount of the check for each public official. If the expenditures are a result of an event at which more than 25 public officials were in attendance, are a result of an event to which an entire standing committee of the legislature was invited in writing to be informed concerning a bill that was assigned to that standing committee, or are a result of an event to which an entire caucus of

either house of the legislature was invited in writing, a lobbyist or a lobbyist agent shall report the total amount expended on the public officials in attendance for food and beverage and is not required to report the amount expended on the public officials individually. In reporting those amounts, the lobbyist or lobbyist agent shall file a statement providing a description by category of the persons in attendance and the nature of each event or function held during the preceding reporting period.

(3) A person who, without good cause, fails to report under subsection (1) shall pay a late filing fee of $10.00 for each day the report remains not filed in violation of subsection (1), not to exceed $300.00. A person who without good cause is in violation of subsection (1) more than 30 days is guilty of a misdemeanor, punishable by a fine of not more than $1,000.00.

(4) If a lobbyist agent employs another lobbyist agent to engage in lobbying, the activities of the employee lobbyist agent shall be reported by the employer lobbyist agent under this section.

(5) Within a reasonable time after receipt of a request from an elected public official in regard to a report of a lobbyist or a lobbyist agent, the secretary of state shall report to the elected public official on any reported activity by the lobbyist or lobbyist agent in that report, and shall notify the elected public official of the specific occurrence and the specific nature of the reported activity.

(6) The secretary of state shall preserve statements and reports filed under this act for 5 years after filing. The statements and reports may be reproduced pursuant to the records media act. After the required preservation period, the statements and reports, or the reproductions of the statements and reports, other than those necessary to complete an investigation by the attorney general or pertinent to a matter being adjudicated in a court of law, shall be destroyed.

4.419 Preservation of accounts, bills, receipts, books, papers, and documents; inspection of records; contents of records; violation; penalty.

Sec. 9.

(1) A lobbyist or a lobbyist agent acting on behalf of the lobbyist, and a lobbyist agent acting on his or her own behalf, shall obtain and preserve all accounts, bills, receipts, books, papers, and documents necessary to substantiate the reports required to be made pursuant to section 8 for 5 years after the report containing those items is filed. These records shall be made available for inspection upon request by the secretary of state after reasonable notice.

(2) A person who violates this section is guilty of a misdemeanor and shall be punished by a fine of not more than $1,000.00, or imprisoned for not more than 90 days, or both, and if the person is other than an individual, the person shall be fined not more than $10,000.00.

4.420 Accounting of lobbying and expenditures; waiver; violation; penalty.

Sec. 10.

A lobbyist agent who is compensated, reimbursed, or otherwise employed by a lobbyist, and whose activities and expenditures must be reported by the employing lobbyist pursuant to section 8, shall provide to the employing lobbyist a full accounting of all lobbying and expenditures required to be reported under this act at least 10 days before the employing lobbyist's report is due to be filed. If the lobbyist agent files an authorized report on behalf of the lobbyist, said accounting is waived. A person who violates this subsection is guilty of a misdemeanor and shall be punished by a fine of not more than $1,000.00.

4.421 Employment of lobbyist agent for compensation contingent on outcome of administrative or legislative action; gifts, loans, or preferential interest rates; selling or utilizing certain information for commercial purpose; compensation or reimbursement of public official engaging in lobbying; violations; penalties.

Sec. 11.

(1) A person shall not be employed as a lobbyist agent for compensation contingent in any manner upon the outcome of an administrative or legislative action. A person who knowingly violates this subsection is guilty of a felony and if the person is an individual shall be punished by a fine of not more than $10,000.00, or imprisoned for not more than 3 years, or both, and if the person is other than an individual shall be punished by a fine of not more than $25,000.00.

(2) A lobbyist or lobbyist agent or anyone acting on behalf of a lobbyist or lobbyist agent shall not give a gift or loan, other than a loan made in the normal course of business by an institution as defined in section 5 of Act No. 319 of the Public Acts of 1969, as amended, a national bank, a branch bank, an insurance company issuing a loan or receiving a mortgage in the normal course of business, a premium finance company, a mortgage company, a small loan company, a state or federal credit union, a savings and loan association chartered by this state or the federal government, or a licensee as defined by Act No. 27 of the Public Acts of the Extra Session of 1950 , as amended. For the purpose of this section, a preferential interest rate shall not be given solely on the basis of the credit applicant being a public official or a member of the public official's immediate family. A person who gives a gift in violation of this subsection is guilty of a misdemeanor if the value of the gift is $3,000.00 or less, and shall be punished by a fine of not more than $5,000.00, or imprisoned for not more than 90 days, or both, and if the person is other than an individual the person shall be fined not more than $10,000.00. A person who knowingly gives a gift in violation of this subsection and the value of the gift is more than $3,000.00 is guilty of a felony and if the person is an individual shall be punished by a fine of not more than $10,000.00, or imprisoned for

not more than 3 years, or both, and if the person is other than an individual shall be punished by a fine of not more than $25,000.00.

(3) Information copied from registration forms or activity reports required by this act or from lists compiled from the forms or reports may not be sold or utilized by any person for any commercial purpose. A person who violates this subsection is subject to a civil penalty of not more than $1,000.00.

(4) A public official, other than an individual who is appointed or elected to a board or commission and is not an ex officio member or prohibited by law from having other employment, shall not accept compensation or reimbursement, other than from the state, for personally engaging in lobbying. A person who violates this subsection is guilty of a misdemeanor and shall be punished by a fine of not more than $1,000.00, or imprisoned for not more than 90 days, or both.

4.422 Summaries of statements and reports.

Sec. 12.

The department 2 times a year and annually shall prepare and publish summaries of the statements and reports received. The summaries shall include a list of the names of the lobbyists and lobbyist agents. The summaries shall be given wide public dissemination.

4.423 Statement or report; determination of filing; deadline for filing; notice of error or omission; notice of failure to file; failure to give notice; making corrections; reporting errors, omissions, or failure to file; copy; investigations and hearings.

Sec. 13.

(1) The secretary of state shall determine whether a statement or report, which is required to be filed under this act, is in fact filed.

(2) A statement or report required to be filed under this act shall be filed not later than 4 p.m. of the day on which it is required to be filed. A statement or report which is postmarked by certified mail not less than 2 days before the deadline for filing shall be considered filed within the prescribed time regardless of when it is actually delivered.

(3) Within 10 days after the deadline for filing a statement or report under this act, the secretary of state shall give notice to the filer by certified mail of an error or omission in the statement or report and shall give notice to a person whom the secretary of state finds probable cause exists that a person is required to file, but who has failed to file, a statement or report. A failure to give notice by the secretary of state under this section is not a defense to a criminal action against the person required to file.

(4) Within 20 days after the report or statement is required to be filed, the filer shall make any corrections in the statement or report filed with the secretary of state.

(5) When 30 days have expired after the deadline for filing a statement or report, the secretary of state shall report errors or omissions which were not corrected and failures to file to the attorney general. A copy of the notice to the attorney general shall be mailed to the person who was required to file or was required to correct errors or omissions.

(6) The secretary of state shall conduct investigations and 1 or more hearings as may be necessary to determine if probable cause exists that a violation of this act has occurred. A hearing conducted pursuant to this subsection shall be in accordance with the procedures set forth in Act No. 306 of the Public Acts of 1969, as amended, being sections 24.201 to 24.315 of the Michigan Compiled Laws.

4.424 Enforcement of penalties; filing sworn complaint; determination of probable cause; notices; cooperation in conduct of investigations.

Sec. 14.

(1) If the secretary of state, upon investigation of a report filed under this act, determines that there is probable cause a violation of this act occurred, the secretary of state shall forward the results of that investigation to the attorney general for enforcement of the penalties provided by this act.

(2) A sworn complaint alleging a violation of this act or the rules promulgated under this act shall be filed with the secretary of state. Upon receipt of a sworn complaint, the attorney general shall determine whether there is probable cause that there was a violation of this act or the rules promulgated under this act. Notice shall be given to a person within 5 days after a sworn complaint is filed against that person. Notice shall include a copy of the sworn complaint. Every 60 days after the date of a request for an investigation and until the matter is terminated, the attorney general shall mail to the complainant and to the alleged violator notice of the action taken to date by the attorney general, together with the reasons for the action or nonaction. If it is determined that there is no probable cause that a violation of this act did occur, the attorney general shall immediately give notice thereof to the complainant and to the person previously given notice under this subsection.

(3) All governmental bodies shall cooperate with the department of attorney general in the conduct of its investigations.

4.425 Ordinance or resolution.

Sec. 15.

A county, city, township, village, or school district may not adopt an ordinance or resolution that is more restrictive than the provisions contained in this act.

4.426 Rules.

Sec. 16.

The secretary of state shall promulgate rules and issue declaratory rules to implement this act pursuant to Act No. 306 of the Public Acts of 1969, as amended.

4.427 Civil action; criminal prosecution.

Sec. 17.

The attorney general upon investigation and determination that this act or a rule promulgated under this act was violated, shall do either of the following:

(a) Initiate a civil action to enforce this act.

(b) Begin criminal prosecution for the imposition of criminal penalties provided by this act in the judicial district in which the alleged violation occurred.

4.428 Severability.

Sec. 18.

If any portion of this act or the application of this act to any person or circumstances is found to be invalid by a court, the invalidity shall not affect the remaining portions or applications of this act which can be given effect without the invalid portion or application, if the remaining portions are not determined by the court to be inoperable.

City of Cincinnati, Ohio Ordinance 0151-1997

As passed by Cincinnati City Council, May 21, 1997

Ordinance 0151-1997 Chapter 112, Council Lobbying

REPEALING existing Chapter 112 and reordaining new Chapter 112 of the Cincinnati Municipal Code to provide a comprehensive plan for the registration of legislative agents and the lobbying of Council.

WHEREAS, in 1980, Council passed Chapter 112 of the Cincinnati Municipal code which dealt with the lobbying of Council in reference to the Cincinnati cable television franchise legislation; and

WHEREAS, it is now timely and appropriate to expand such legislation to place controls on the lobbying of any member of the councilor appointee of the council, the city manager, the department directors, or any member of the staff of any public officer or employee, over all City matters and to provide procedures for the registration of legislative agents; and

WHEREAS the State of Ohio has in place comprehensive legislation which requires registration of legislative agents of the General Assembly, and the filing of statements of expenditures concerning the lobbying of member of the General Assembly; and

WHEREAS, Council find that the State of Ohio lobbying regulations provide a model for such local regulations; and

WHEREAS, Council find that the enactment of current legislation requiring the registration of legislative agents and the disclosure of their employers, and also the filing of statements making public the financial transactions that may be used to influence Council legislation and hence the policies of the City, is necessary and appropriate and will lead to a better governed City of Cincinnati; now, therefore.

BE IT ORDAINED by the Council of the City of Cincinnati, State of Ohio

Section 1. That Chapter 112 of the Cincinnati Municipal Code currently in effect is repealed.

Section 2. That new Chapter 112 of the Cincinnati Municipal Code is reordained to read as follows: **197**

CHAPTER 112 COUNCIL LOBBYING

Author'sNote: The statistics published below are
matter of public record and were obtained from the City Hall
In Los Angeles, California

A COMPREHENSIVE LOBBYING REPORT

The City of Los Angeles established it's own City Ethics Commission
and reports quarterly to the City Council and to all interested citizens.
The information offered below is public information. It is offered here only as
an accurate record of the size and scope of lobbying in a large city.

The report referred to is for the period of June 2, 2000. It will
include both a list of registered lobbyists and a list of registered clients.
Lobbying reports for that period indicate that the ten projects that clients paid
the most fees for the first quarter of 2000 for municipal lobbying activities
were:

Lobbying Fees Paid

1. Open Access/Broadband	$248,858
2. Playa Vista Project	165,275
3. Expansion Pico/Doheny Oil	155,580
4. Duty Free Stores Contract	119,605
5. Greek Theater Contract	99,358
6. Farmers Market project	89,619

7. Hollywood/Highland project $ 87,559

8. Warner Center Project   85,376

9. Home Depot projects   85,079

10. Sunset Millennium project   82,462

A description of each of the above projects follows in the complete report, giving the background and an individual accounting of the lobbying fees paid by the client in toto.

A further breakdown is given of fees paid to one or more lobbying firms.

We include as examples, a few of the above projects as follows:

Project: OPEN ACCESS/BROADBAND

Client: AT & T

Client Payments on Issue	$169,991
Rose Kindel	$60,000
Cerrell Associates, Inc	$37,238
Afriat Consulting Group	$31,049
The MWW Group	$21,000
Strategy Workshop	$14,700

Client: Open Access Alliance

Client Payments on Issue	$15,390

Dakota Communications	$15,390

Client: Los Angeles Cable Assn.

Client Payments on Issue	$11,942
Afriat Consulting Group	$11,842

Client: America Online, Inc.

Client Payments on Issue	$1,290
Latham & Watkins $1,290	

PLAYA VISTA PROJECT

Client: Playa Vista Co, LLC

Client Payments on Issue	$165,275.

Mannat Phelps,Phillips	$75,550
Kelly, Lytton, Mintz	$37,000
Psomas & Assoc.	$30,887
Playa Capital in house lobbyists $11,963	
Latham & Watkins	$8,875

DUTY FREE STORES CONTRACT

Client: World Duty Free Americas

Client Payments on Issue	$76,000
Rose & Kindel	$60,000
Katherine Moret	$16,000

Client: DFS North America $ 43,605

Diverse Strategies $ 25,000

Cerrell Associates $10,105

Manatt Phelps, Phllips   ` $ 8,500

GREEK THEATRE CONTRACT

Client: House of Blues Concerts

Client Payments on Issue $50,985

Dakota Communications $30,287

Latham & Watkins $15,095

Afriat Consulting Group $5,603

Client: Nederlander-Greek, Inc.

Client Payments on Issue $48,873

Iverson, Yoakum ,Papiano $46,873

Ken Spiker & Assoc. $1,500

HOME DEPOT PROJECTS

Client: Home Depot

Client Payments on Issue: $85,079

The McCarty Co $57,03

Consensus

Planning Group $28,040

The number of lobbyists and clients registering with the City Ethics Commission has increased steadily since the Lobbying Ordinance was amended in 1995. During the first quarter 2000, 152 lobbyists and 468 clients registered with the Commission. This represents an increase of 15 lobbyists and 95 clients compared to the same period last year.

Number of Registered Lobbyists   152

Number of Registered Lobbying firms   60

Number of Registered Lobbyist Employers   13

Number of Registered clients   468

LOBBYING EXPENDITURES for the first quarter of 2000 totaled $2,121,059

Payments to lobbyists $1,239,114

Payments to other employees

For related lobbying activity $31,520

Activity Expenses $49,443

Other Expenses made to influence

Municipal legislation-- $490,982

TEXT OF TITLE 2, UNITED STATES CODE - SECTIONS 160L - 1612

The Lobbying Disclosure Act of 1995, as Amended, by the Lobbying Disclosure Technical Amendments Act of 1998

The Congress finds that (1) responsible representative Government requires public awareness of the efforts of paid lobbyists to influence the public decision making process in both the legislative and executive branches of the Federal Government.

(1)   existing lobbying disclosure statutes have been ineffective because of unclear statutory language, weak administration and enforcement provisions, and an absence of clear guidance as to who is required to register and what they are required to disclose, and

(2)   the effective public disclosure of the identity and extent of the efforts of paid lobbyists to influence Federal officials in the conduct of Government actions will increase public confidence in the integrity of government.

Note: complete text of Federal Law available upon request. Small repro cost. (approximately 18 pages)

To Order Additional Copies of

EVERYBODY LOBBIES
Write to

The Lobby Channel
19864 N. 68th Dr.
Glendale, AZ 85308

GLENDALE, AZ.   85308

Or call: 623-566-9531

Website (under construction)
www.thelobbychannel.com